777 REVISED

ISBN: 978-1-63923-514-8

Printed: October 2022

Cover Art By: Amit Paul

Published and Distributed By:
Lushena Books
607 Country Club Drive, Unit E
Bensenville, IL 60106
www.lushenabks.com

ISBN: 978-1-63923-514-8

777 REVISED

VEL PROLEGOMENA SYMBOLICA AD SYSTEMAM
SCEPTICO-MYSTICÆ VIÆ EXPLICANDÆ,
FVNDAMENTVM HIEROGLYPHICVM SANCTISSI-
MORVM SCIENTIÆ SVMMÆ

אחת רוח אלהים חיים

A REPRINT OF 777
WITH MUCH ADDITIONAL MATTER
BY THE LATE

ALEISTER CROWLEY

LIBER DCCLXXVII. A COMPLETE DICTIONARY OF THE CORRESPONDENCES OF ALL MAGICAL ELEMENTS, reprinted with extensive additions, making it the only standard comprehensive book of reference ever published. It is to the language of Occultism what Webster or Murray is to the English language.

"Præmonstrance of A∴A∴," *Equinox* III (1).

CONTENTS

* EDITORIAL PREFACE (to *777 Revised*) vi

INTRODUCTION (from the first edition) xi

THE TREE OF LIFE xviii

TABLES OF CORRESPONDENCE 1

    TABLE I: The whole scale 2

    TABLE II: The Elements 18

    TABLE III: The Planets 20

    TABLE IV: The Sephiroth 21

    TABLE V: The Zodiac 26

    TABLE VI: The Paths 33

* VARIOUS ARRANGEMENTS 36

NOTES TO TABLES OF CORRESPONDENCE 42

APPENDIX: THE YI KING 49

* EXPLANATIONS OF THE ATTRIBUTIONS 59

* THE NATURE AND SIGNIFICANCE OF THE MAGICAL ALPHABET 124

* BRIEF MEANINGS OF THE PRIMES 132

* WHAT IS QABALAH? 133

* WHAT IS A "NUMBER" OR "SYMBOL"? 134

EDITORIAL PREFACE*

777 is a qabalistic dictionary of ceremonial magic, oriental mysticism, comparative religion, and symbology. It is also a handbook for ceremonial invocation and for checking the validity of dreams and visions. It is indispendisble to those who wish to correlate these apparently diverse studies. It was published privately by Aleister Crowley in 1909, has long been out of print and is now practically unprocurable.

Crowley, who had a phenomenal memory, wrote it at Bournemouth in a week without reference books—or so he claimed in an unpublished section of his "Confessions."† It is not, however, entirely original. Ninety per cent of the Hebrew, the four colour scales, and the order and attribution of the Tarot trumps are as taught in the Hermetic Order of the Golden Dawn with its inner circle of the Rose of Ruby and the Cross of Gold (R.R. et A.C.)

This Order is still in existence, though it has changed its name and is dormant, for it no longer accepts probationers.‡ It was the

---

* [This preface appeared in the 1955 first edition of *777 Revised* and is believed to be by Gerald Yorke (Frater V.I.) who edited the revised edition. — T.S.]

† [Published in a slightly abridged form as *The Confessions of Aleister Crowley* edited by John Symonds and Kenneth Grant, London, Jonathan Cape, 1969; reprinted Harmandsworth, Penguin Arkana, 1989. The passage in question appears at the end of chapter 59 of this edition (p. 533). — T.S.]

‡ [Yorke may have been alluding to the Alpha et Omega, which was the name adopted by that part of the G.D. which remained loyal to Mathers shortly after the split. It went into dormancy after the G.D. rituals and Knowledge Lectures were published in 1937-40 by F.I. Regardie, an expelled former member of the Stella Matutina (the other main group to emerge from the split). At the time of writing a number of groups claiming to be or claiming derivation from the Golden Dawn are in existence, some recruiting more or less openly (one has

fountain head from which Crowley and W.B. Yeats drank in their twenties. In this school they learned the traditional Western symbolism which coloured so much of their poetry and their thought. In it they were taught ceremonial magic, how to skry, and the technique for exploring the subtler realms of the mind on the so-called "astral plane."

Crowley, however, was not content with the traditional qabalistic teaching of this Western Heremetic Order with its stress on magic and demonology. He travelled eastwards, becoming a fair Arabic scholar and studying the Mahommedan secret tradition under a qualified teacher in Cairo. Going on to India he learned the elements of Shaivite Yoga at the feet of Sri Parananda, who was Solicitor-General of Ceylon before he became a sadhu. In Southern India he studied Vedanta and Raja Yoga with "the Mahatma Jnana Guru Yogi Sabhapaty Swami." He was thus qualified to equate the Hindu and Qabalistic systems.

Allan Bennett, his friend and teacher in the Golden Dawn, had become the Burmese Buddhist bhikkhu Ananda Metteya. Crowley studied under him both in Ceylon and Burmah, and so was able to add the Hinayana* Buddhist columns to 777. Although he walked eastwards into China he never found a qualified teacher of Taoism or the Yi King. His attributions of the trigrams to the Tree of Life and his explanation of the hexagrams in Appendix I to 777 were based on Legge's translation.

Crowley was 32 when he wrote 777. Later as his knowledge and experience widened he became increasingly dissatisfied with it. He planned an enlarged edition which would correct a few errors, incorporate much new material, and bring the whole into line with The Book of the Law. He worked on this in the nineteen

---

even gone to the lengths of trademarking the name and emblems of the order).
I will not here comment on such claims. — T.S.]
* [More normally known as Therevada. Hinayana ("lesser path") is an abusive epiphet used by followers of the "Mahayana" school for those who do not accept their elaborations and admixtures. — T.S.]

twenties, but never completed it. What he did finish is published here—most of it for the first time. The task of editing has been restricted for the most part to the omission of incomplete notes.

The new material, which is marked with an asterisk in the Table of Contents, consists of an essay on the magical alphabet, a short note on Qabalah and a new theory on number. Then the more important columns in Table I are explained. These explanations include a few corrections and a number of important additions to the original Table. Those who wish to work with these Tables should extract the additions from the text, and add them to the appropriate lines of the column concerned.* Finally some new columns and "arrangements" have been included, partly from *The Book of Thoth*, and partly from holograph notes in Crowley's own *777*. The editor has assumed that Crowley intended to incorporate these in the new edition. For the few interested in Gematria the numerical values of the Greek and Arabic alphabets have been added.†

Crowley never completed *777 Revised*, but he left enough material to justify its posthumous publication.

N∴

---

* [This has already been done in the re-set version of the Tables which follow. These additions are distinguished by being in double square brackets [[like this]]. Further, the additional columns from *777 Revised* have been integrated into the main table. See my notes at the end for a more detailed discussion of this treatment. — T.S.]

† [In the re-set Tables following, numeration of Coptic has also been added.]

LIBER 777

VEL
PROLEGOMENA
SYMBOLICA
AD SYSTEMAM
SCEPTICO-MYSTICÆ
VIÆ EXPLICANDÆ
FUNDAMENTUM
HIEROGLYPHICUM
SANCTISSIMORUM
SCIENTÆ SUMMÆ

A∴A∴
publication in Class B

IMPRIMATUR

V.V.V.V.V.	8°=3▫	Pro Collegio Summo.
D.D.S.	7°=4▫	} Pro Collegio Interno.
O.M.	7°=4▫	
V.N.	5°=6▫	
P.A.	5°=6▫	} Pro Collegio Externo.
P.	4°=7▫	

777

THE FOLLOWING is an attempt to systematise alike the data of mysticism and the results of comparative religion.

The sceptic will applaud our labours, for that the very catholicity of the symbols denies them any objective validity, since, in so many contradictions, something must be false; while the mystic will rejoice equally that the self-same catholicity all-embracing proves that very validity, since after all something must be true.

Fortunately we have learnt to combine these ideas, not in the mutual toleration of sub-contraries, but in the affirmation of contraries, that transcending of the laws of intellect which is madness in the ordinary man, genius in the Overman who hath arrived to strike off more fetters from our understanding. The savage who cannot conceive of the number six, the orthodox mathematician who cannot conceive of the fourth dimension, the philosopher who cannot conceive of the Absolute—all these are one; all must be impregnated with the Divine Essence of the Phallic Yod of Macroprosopus, and give birth to their idea. True (we may agree with Balzac), the Absolute recedes; we never grasp it; but in the travelling there is joy. Am I no better than a staphylococcus because my ideas still crowd in chains?

But we digress.

The last attempts to tabulate knowledge are the *Kabbala Denudata* of Knorr von Rosenroth (a work incomplete and, in some of its parts, prostituted to the service of dogmatic interpretation), the lost symbolism of the Vault in which Christian

Rosenkreutz is said to have been buried, some of the work of Dr. Dee and Sir Edward Kelly, some very imperfect tables in Cornelius Agrippa, the "Art" of Raymond Lully, some of the very artificial effusions of the esoteric Theosophists, and of late years the knowledge of the Order Rosæ Rubeæ et Aureæ Crucis and the Hermetic Order of the Golden Dawn. Unluckily, the leading spirit in these latter societies[1]* found that his prayer, "Give us this day our daily whisky, and just a wee drappie mair for luck!" was sternly answered, "When you have given us this day our daily Knowledge-lecture."

Under these circumstances Daath got mixed with Dewar, and Beelzebub with Buchanan.

But even the best of these systems is excessively bulky; modern methods have enabled us to concentrate the substance of twenty thousand pages in two score.

The best of the serious attempts to systematise the results of Comparative Religion is that made by Blavatsky. But though she had an immense genius for acquiring facts, she had none whatever for sorting and selecting the essentials.

Grant Allen made a very slipshod experiment in this line; so have some of the polemical rationalists; but the only man worthy of our notice is Frazer of the *Golden Bough*. Here again, there is no tabulation;[2] for us it is left to sacrifice literary charm, and even some accuracy, in order to bring out the one great point.

This: That when a Japanese thinks of Hachiman, and a Boer of the Lord of Hosts, they are not two thoughts, but one.

The cause of human sectarianism is not lack of sympathy in thought, but in speech; and this it is our not unambitious design to remedy.

Every new sect aggravates the situation. Especially the Americans, grossly and crapulously ignorant as they are of the rudiments of human language, seize like mongrel curs upon the

---

* [Notes indicated by numbers—due to the present transcriber—are found at the end of this volume. — T.S.]

putrid bones of their decaying monkey-jabber, and gnaw and tear them with fierce growls and howls.

The mental prostitute, Mrs. Eddy (for example), having invented the idea which ordinary people call "God," christened it "Mind," and then by affirming a set of propositions about "Mind," which are only true of "God," set all hysterical, dyspeptic, crazy Amurrka by the ears. Personally, I don't object to people discussing the properties of four-sided triangles; but I draw the line when they use a well-known word, such as pig, or mental healer, or dung-heap, to denote the object of their paranoiac fetishism.

Even among serious philosophers the confusion is very great. Such terms as God, the Absolute, Spirit, have dozens of connotations, according to the time and place of the dispute and the beliefs of the disputants.

Time enough that these definitions and their inter-relation should be crystallised, even at the expense of accepted philosophical accuracy.

2. The principal sources of our tables have been the philosophers and traditional systems referred to above, as also, among many others, Pietri di Abano,[3] Lilly, Eliphaz Levi, Sir R. Burton, Swami Vivekananda, the Hindu, Buddhist, and Chinese Classics, the Qúran and its commentators, the Book of the Dead, and, in particular, original research. The Chinese, Hindu, Buddhist, Moslem and Egyptian systems have never before been brought into line with the Qabalah; the Tarot has never been made public.

Eliphaz Levi knew the true attributions but was forbidden to use them.*

All this secrecy is very silly. An indicible Arcanum is an arcanum that *cannot* be revealed. It is simply bad faith to swear a man to the most horrible penalties if he betray . . ., etc., and then take him mysteriously apart and confide the Hebrew Alphabet to his safe keeping.[4] This is perhaps only ridiculous; but it is a

---

* This is probably true, though in agreement with the statement of the traducer of Levi's doctrine and the vilifier of his noble personality.

wicked imposture to pretend to have received it from Rosicrucian manuscripts which are to be found in the British Museum. To obtain money on these grounds, as has been done by certain moderns, is clear (and, I trust, indictable) fraud.

The secrets of Adepts are not to be revealed to men. We only wish they were. When a man comes to me and asks for the Truth, I go away and practice teaching the Differential Calculus to a Bushman; and I answer the former only when I have succeeded with the latter. But to withhold the Alphabet of Mysticism from the learner is the device of a selfish charlatan. That which can be taught shall be taught, and that which cannot be taught may at last be learnt.

3. As a weary but victorious warrior delights to recall his battles—Fortisan hæc olim meminisse juvabit*—we would linger for a moment upon the difficulties of our task.

The question of sacred alphabets has been abandoned as hopeless. As one who should probe the nature of woman, the deeper he goes the rottener it gets; so that at last it is seen that there is no sound bottom. All is arbitrary;† withdrawing out caustics and adopting a protective treatment, we point to the beautiful clean bandages and ask the clinic to admire! To take one concrete example: the English T is clearly equivalent in sound to the Hebrew ‎ת‎, the Greek τ, the Arabic ﺕ and the Coptic τ, but the numeration is not the same. Again, we have a clear analogy in shape (perhaps a whole series of analogies), which, on comparing the modern alphabets with primeval examples, breaks up and is indecipherable.

---

* [*Lat.* approx. "perhaps it will be pleasant to remember these things one day."]
† All symbolism is perhaps ultimately so; there is no necessary relation in thought between the idea of a mother, the sound of the child's cry "Ma," and the combination of lines *ma*. This, too, is the extreme case, since "ma" is the sound naturally just produced by opening the lips and breathing. Hindus would make a great fuss over this true connection; but it is very nearly the only one. All these beautiful schemes break down sooner or later, mostly sooner.

The same difficulty in another form permeates the question of gods.

Priests, to propitiate their local fetish, would flatter him with the title of creator; philosophers, with a wider outlook, would draw identities between many gods in order to obtain a unity. Time and the gregarious nature of man have raised gods as ideas grew more universal; sectarianism has drawn false distinctions between identical gods for polemical purposes.

Thus, where shall we put Isis, favouring nymph of corn as she was? As the type of motherhood? As the moon? As the great goddess Earth? As Nature? As the Cosmic Egg from which all Nature sprang? For as time and place have changed, so she is all of these!

What of Jehovah, that testy senior of Genesis, that lawgiver of Leviticus, that Phallus of the depopulated slaves of the Egyptians, that jealous King-God of the times of the Kings, that more spiritual conception of the Captivity, only invented when all temporal hope was lost, that mediæval battleground of cross-chopped logic, that Being stripped of all his attributes and assimilated to Parabrahman and the Absolute of the Philosopher?

Satan, again, who in Job is merely Attorney-General and prosecutes for the Crown, acquires in time all the obloquy attaching to that functionary in the eyes of the criminal classes, and becomes a slanderer. Does any one really think that any angel is such a fool as to try to gull the Omniscient God into injustice to his saints?

Then, on the other hand, what of Moloch, that form of Jehovah denounced by those who did not draw huge profit from his rites? What of the savage and morose Jesus of the Evangelicals, cut by their petty malice from the gentle Jesus of the Italian children? How shall we identify the thaumaturgic Chauvinist of Matthew with the metaphysical Logos of John? In short, while the human mind is mobile, so long will the definitions of all our terms vary.

But it is necessary to settle on something: bad rules are better than no rules at all. We may then hope that our critics will aid our acknowledged feebleness; and if it be agreed that much learning hath made us mad, that we may receive humane treatment and a liberal allowance of rubber-cores in our old age.

4. The Tree of Life is the skeleton on which this body of truth is built. The juxtaposition and proportion of its parts should be fully studied. Practice alone will enable the student to determine how far an analogy may be followed out. Again, some analogies may escape a superficial study. The Beetle is only connected with the sign Pisces through the Tarot Trump "The Moon." The Camel is only connected with the High Priestess through the letter Gimel.

Since all things whatsoever (including no thing) may be placed upon the Tree of Life, the Table could never be complete. It is already somewhat unwieldy; we have tried to confine ourselves as far as possible to lists of Things Generally Unknown. It must be remembered that the lesser tables are only divided from the thirty-two-fold table in order to economise space; *e.g.* in the seven-fold table the entries under Saturn belong to the thirty-second part in the large table.

We have been unable for the moment to tabulate many great systems of Magic; the four lesser books of the Lemegeton,[5] the system of Abramelin, if indeed its Qliphothic ramifications are susceptible of classification, once we follow it below the great and terrible Demonic Triads which are under the presidency of the Unutterable Name;[6] the vast and comprehensive system shadowed in the Book called the Book of the Concourse of the Forces,[7] interwoven as it is with the Tarot, being, indeed, on one view little more than an amplification and practical application of the Book of Thoth.[8]

But we hope that the present venture will attract scholars from all quarters, as when the wounded Satan leaned upon his spear,

" Forthwith on all sides to his aid was run
By angels many and strong,"

and that in the course of time a far more satisfactory volume may result.

Many columns will seem to the majority of people to consist of mere lists of senseless words. Practice, and advance in the magical or mystical path, will enable little by little to interpret more and more.

Even as a flower unfolds beneath the ardent kisses of the Sun, so will this table reveal its glories to the dazzling eye of illumination. Symbolic and barren as it is, yet it shall stand for the athletic student as a perfect sacrament, so that reverently closing its pages he shall exclaim, "May that of which we have partaken sustain us in the search for the Quintessence, the Stone of the Wise, the Summum Bonus, True Wisdom, and Perfect Happiness."

So mote it be!

THE TREE OF LIFE

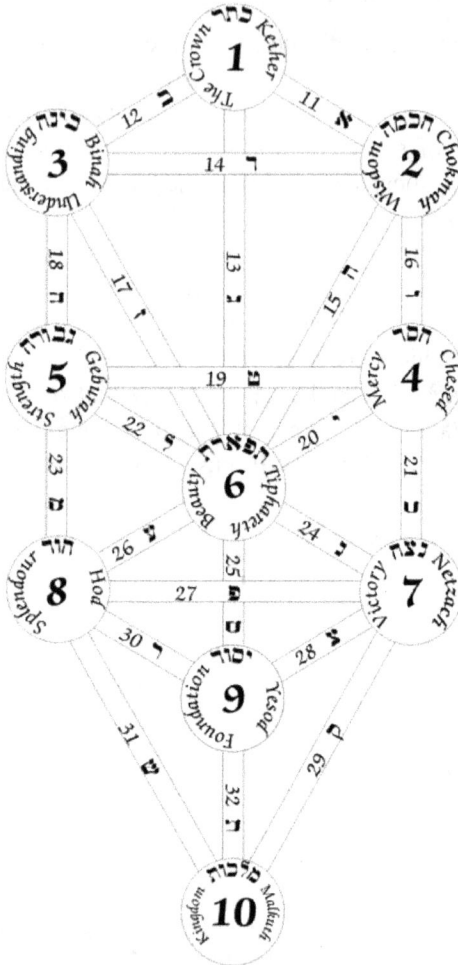

COL. XII. This arrangement is the basis of the whole system of this book. Besides the 10 numbers and the 22 letters, it is divisible into 3 columns, 4 planes, 7 planes, 7 palaces, etc. etc.

TABLE OF
CORRESPONDENCES

I. Key Scale.	II.* Hebrew Names of Numbers and Letters.		III. English of Col. II.	IV.* Consciousness of the Adept.	V.* God-Names in Assiah.
0	אין	Ain	Nothing	. . . .	
	אין סוף	Ain Soph	No Limit		
	אין סוף אור	Ain Soph Aur	Limitless L.V.X		
1	כתר *	Kether	Crown*	הוא	אהיה
2	חכמה *	Chokmah	Wisdom		יה
3	בינה *	Binah	Understanding		יהוה אלהים
4	חסד *	Chesed	Mercy		אל
5	גבורה *	Geburah	Strength		אלהים גבור
6	תפארת *	Tiphareth	Beauty		יהוה אלוה ודעת
7	נצח	Netzach	Victory		יהוה צבאות
8	הוד	Hod	Splendour		אלהים צבאות
9	יסוד *	Yesod	Foundation		שדי אל חי
10	מלכות *	Malkuth	Kingdom		אדני מלך
11	אלף	Aleph	Ox		יהוה
12	בית	Beth	House		אזבוגה (8)
13	גמל	Gimel	Camel		(81) דה (9) אלים
14	דלת	Daleth	Door		(7) אהא
15	הה	Hé	Window		
16	וו	Vau	Nail		
17	זין	Zain	Sword		
18	חית	Cheth	Fence		
19	טית	Teth	Serpent		
20	יוד	Yod	Hand		
21	כף	Kaph	Palm		(34) אל אב (4) אבא
22	למד	Lamed	Ox Goad		אל
23	מים	Maim	Water		
24	נון	Nun	Fish		
25	סמך	Samekh	Prop		
26	עין	Ayin	Eye		
27	פה	Pé	Mouth		(65) אדני
28	צדי	Tzaddi	Fish-hook		
29	קוף	Qoph	Back of head		
30	ריש	Resh	Head		(36) אלה
31	שין	Shin	Tooth		אלהים
32	תו	Tau	Tau (as Egyptian)		(15) יה (3) אב
32 bis	תו	Tau	. . . .		[האריץ] אדני
31 bis	שין	Shin	. . . .		[אהיה : אגלא] יהשוה

[Asterisks indicate that there is further information concerning the column or individual entry in the notes on pp. 42-48.]

TABLE I (*continued*) 3

	VI. The Heavens of Assiah.		VII. English of Col. VI.	VIII.* Orders of Qliphoth.	
0	. . . .		. . . .	. . . .	
1	הגלגלים ראשית	Rashith ha-Gilgalim	Sphere of Primum Mobile	תאומיאל (1)	Thaumiel
2	מזלות	Mazloth	Sphere of the Zodiac	עוגיאל (1)	Ghagiel
3	שבתאי	Shabbathai	Sphere of Saturn	(1) סאתאריאל	Satariel
4	צדק	Tzedeq	Sphere of Jupiter	גּעשכלה (2)	Gha'agsheklah
5	מאדים	Madim	Sphere of Mars	גולחב (3)	Golachab
6	שמש	Shemesh	Sphere of Sol	תגרירון (4)	Thagiriron
7	נגה	Nogah	Sphere of Venus	ערב זרק (5)	A'arab Zaraq
8	כוכב	Kokab	Sphere of Mercury	סמאל (6)	Samael
9	לבנה	Levanah	Sphere of Luna	גמיאל (7)	Gamaliel
10	חלם יסודות	Cholem Yesodoth	Sphere of the Elements	לילית (7)	Lilith
11	רוח	Ruach	Air	[Elements. See Col. LXVIII.]	
12	[Planets follow Sephiroth, corresponding]		Mercury	[Planets follow Sephiroth]	
13	. . . .		Luna	. . . .	
14	. . . .		Venus	. . . .	
15	תלה	Teleh	Aries △	בעירירון *	Ba'airiron
16	שור	Shar	Taurus ▽	אדימירון	Adimiron
17	תאונים	Teonim	Gemini	צללימירון	Tzalalimiron
18	סרטן	Sarton	Cancer ▽	שיחתירון	Shichiriron
19	אריה	Ari	Leo △	שלהבירון	Shalehbiron
20	בתולה	Betulah	Virgo ▽	צפירירון	Tzaphiriron
21	. . . .		Jupiter	. . . .	
22	מאזנים	Moznaim	Libra △	עבירירון	A'abiriron
23	מים	Maim	Water	. . . .	
24	עקרב	Akrab	Scorpio ▽	נחשתירון	Necheshthiron
25	קשת	Qesheth	Sagittarius △	נחשירון	Necheshiron
26	גדי	Gedi	Capricorn ▽	דגדגירון	Dagdagiron
27	. . . .		Mars	. . . .	
28	דלי	Deli	Aquarius △	בהימירון	Bahimiron
29	דגים	Dagim	Pisces ▽	נשימירון	Nashimiron
30	. . . .		Sol	. . . .	
31	אש	Ash	Fire	. . . .	
32	. . . .		Saturn	. . . .	
32 bis	ארץ	Aretz	Earth	. . . .	
31 bis	את	Ath	Spirit	. . . .	

	IX. The Sword and the Serpent	X. Mystic Numbers of the Sephiroth	XI.* Elements (with their Planetary Rulers).	XII.* The Tree of Life.
0	. . . . . .	0	. . . . . .	. . . . . .
1		1	Root of 🜁	1st Plane, Middle Pillar
2		3	Root of △	2nd Plane, Right Pillar
3		6	Root of ▽	2nd Plane, Left Pillar
4	The Flaming Sword follows the downward course of the Sephiroth, and is compared to the Lightning Flash. Its hilt is in Kether and its point in Malkuth.	10	▽	3rd Plane, Right Pillar
5		15	△	3rd Plane, Left Pillar
6		21	🜁	4th Plane, Middle Pillar
7		28	△	5th Plane, Right Pillar
8		36	▽	5th Plane, Left Pillar
9		45	🜁	6th Plane, Middle Pillar
10		55	🜃	7th Plane, Middle Pillar
11		66	Hot and Moist 🜁	Path joins 1 – 2
12		78	. . . . . .	,, 1 – 3
13		91	. . . . . .	,, 1 – 6
14		105	. . . . . .	,, 2 – 3
15		120	☉ △ ♃	,, 2 – 6
16		136	♀ ▽ ☽	,, 2 – 4
17		153	♄ 🜁 ☿	,, 3 – 6
18	The Serpent of Wisdom follows the course of the paths or letters upwards, its head being thus in ש, its tail in ת. א, ה, מ, and ש are the Mother letters, referring to the Elements; ב, ג, ד, כ, פ, ר, and ת, the Double letters, to the Planets; the rest, Single letters, to the Zodiac.	171	♂ ▽	,, 3 – 5
19		190	☉ △ ♃	,, 4 – 5
20		210	♀ ▽ ☽	,, 4 – 6
21		231	. . . . . .	,, 4 – 7
22		253	♄ 🜁 ☿	,, 5 – 6
23		276	Cold and moist ▽	,, 5 – 8
24		300	♂ ▽	,, 6 – 7
25		325	☉ △ ♃	,, 6 – 9
26		351	♀ ▽ ☽	,, 6 – 8
27		378	. . . . . .	,, 7 – 8
28		406	♄ 🜁 ☿	,, 7 – 9
29		435	♂ ▽	,, 7 – 10
30		465	. . . . . .	,, 8 – 9
31		496	Hot and dry △	,, 8 – 10
32		528	. . . . . .	,, 9 – 10
32 bis	. . . . . .		Cold and dry 🜃	. . . . . .
31 bis	. . . . . .			. . . . . .

TABLE I (*continued*) 5

	XIII. The Paths of the Sepher Yetzirah.	XIV. General Attribution of Tarot.	XV.* The King Scale of Colour (*).
0	. . . .	. . . .	. . . .
1	Admirable or Hidden Intelligence	The 4 Aces	Brilliance
2	Illuminating I.	The 4 Twos—Kings or Knights	Pure soft blue
3	Sanctifying I.	The 4 Threes—Queens	Crimson
4	Measuring Cohesive or Receptacular I.	The 4 Fours	Deep violet
5	Radical I.	The 4 Fives	Orange
6	I. of the Mediating Influence	The 4 Sixes—Emperors or Princes	Clear pink rose
7	Occult or Hidden I.	The 4 Sevens	Amber
8	Absolute or Perfect I.	The 4 Eights	Violet purple
9	Pure or Clear I.	The 4 Nines	Indigo
10	Resplendent I.	The 4 Tens—Empresses or Princesses	Yellow
11	Scintillating I.	The Fool—[Swords] Emperors or Princes	Bright pale yellow
12	I. of Transparency	The Juggler	Yellow
13	Uniting I.	The High Priestess	Blue
14	Illuminating I.	The Empress	Emerald green
15	Constituting I.	The Emperor	Scarlet
16	Triumphal or Eternal One	The Hierophant	Red orange
17	Disposing One	The Lovers	Orange
18	I. of the House of Influence	The Chariot	Amber
19	I. of all the Activities of the Spiritual Being	Strength	Yellow, greenish
20	I. of Will	Hermit	Green, yellowish
21	I. of Conciliation	Wheel of Fortune	Violet
22	Faithful I.	Justice	Emerald green
23	Stable I.	The Hanged Man—[Cups] Queens.	Deep blue
24	Imaginative I.	Death	Green blue
25	I. of Probation or Tentative One	Temperence	Blue
26	Renovating I.	The Devil	Indigo
27	Exciting I.	The House of God	Scarlet
28	Natural I.	The Star	Violet
29	Corporeal I.	The Moon	Crimson (ultra violet)
30	Collecting I.	The Sun	Orange
31	Perpetual I.	The Angel or Last Judgement—[Wands] Kings or Knights.	Glowing orange scarlet
32	Administrative I.	The Universe	Indigo
32 bis	. . . .	Empresses [Coins]	Citrine, russet, olive, and black (quartered)
31 bis	. . . .	All 22 Trumps	White, merging Grey

	XVI.* The Queen Scale of Colour (ה).	XVII.* The Emperor Scale of Colour (ו).	XVIII.* The Empress Scale of Colour (ה).
0	. . . .	. . . .	. . . .
1	White brilliance	White brilliance	White flecked gold
2	Grey	Blue pearl grey, like mother-of pearl	White, flecked red, blue, and yellow
3	Black	Dark brown	Grey flecked pink
4	Blue	Deep purple	Deep azure flecked yellow
5	Scarlet red	Bright scarlet	Red flecked black
6	Yellow (gold)	Rich salmon	Gold amber
7	Emerald	Bright yellow green	Olive flecked gold
8	Orange	Red-russet	Yellow-brown flecked white
9	Violet	Very dark purple	Citrine flecked azure
10	Citrine, olive, russet, and black*	As Queen scale, but flecked with gold	Black rayed yellow
11	Sky blue	Blue emerald green	Emerald flecked gold
12	Purple	Grey	Indigo rayed violet
13	Silver	Cold pale blue	Silver rayed sky-blue
14	Sky blue	Early spring green	Bright rose of cerise rayed pale yellow
15	Red	Brilliant flame	Glowing red
16	Deep indigo	Deep warm olive	Rich brown
17	Pale Mauve	New yellow leather	Reddish grey inclined to mauve
18	Maroon	Rich bright russet	Dark greenish brown
19	Deep purple	Grey	Reddish amber
20	Slate grey	Green grey	Plum colour
21	Blue	Rich purple	Bright blue rayed yellow
22	Blue	Deep blue-green	Pale green
23	Sea-green	Deep olive-green	White flecked purple
24	Dull brown	Very dark brown	Livid indigo brown (like a black beetle)
25	Yellow	Green	Dark vivid blue
26	Black	Blue black	Cold dark grey near black
27	Red	Venetian red	Bright red rayed azure or orange
28	Sky blue	Blueish mauve	White tinged purple
29	Buff, flecked silver-white	Light translucent pinksh brown	Stone colour
30	Gold yellow	Rich amber	Amber rayed red
31	Vermillion	Scarlet, flecked gold	Vermillion flecked crimson & emerald
32	Black	Blue black	Black rayed blue
32 bis	Amber	Dark brown	Black and yellow
31 bis	Deep purple (near black)	The 7 prismatic colours, the violet being outside	White, red, yellow, blue, black (the latter outside)

TABLE I (*continued*)   7

	XIX.* Selection of Egyptian Gods.	XX. Complete Practical Attribution of Egyptian Gods.	XXI.* The Perfected Man.
0	Harpocrates, Amoun, Nuith [[Nuit and Hadit]]	Heru-pa-Kraath	Nu—the Hair
1	Ptah, Asar un Nefer, Hadith [[Heru-Ra-Ha]]	Ptah	} Disk (of Ra)—the Face.
2	Amoun, Thoth, Nuith [Zodiac]	Isis [As Wisdom]	} [In Daath, Asi—the Neck]
3	Maut, Isis, Nephthys	Nephthys	
4	Amoun, Isis [[Hathoor]]	Amoun	} Neith—the Arms
5	Horus, Nephthys	Horus	}
6	Asar, Ra [[On, Hrumachis]]	Ra	The Mighty and Terrible One—the Breast
7	Hathoor	Hathoor	} The Lords of Kereba—the Reins. Nuit—the Hips and Legs.
8	Anubis	Thoth	
9	Shu [[Hermanubis, all exclusively phallic Gods]]	Shu	Asar and Asi—the Phallus and Vulva. Sati—the Spine
10	Seb. Lower (*i.e.* unwedded) Isis and Nephthys. [[Sphinx as synthesis of Elements]]	Osiris	The Eye of Hoor—the Buttocks and Anus
11	Nu [[Hoor-pa-kraat as ATU 0]]	Mout	As 6
12	Thoth and Cynocephalus	Thoth	Anpu—the Lips
13	Chomse	Chomse	Hathor—the Left Eye
14	Hathor	Hathoor	Khenti-Khas—the Left Nostril
15	Men Thu	Isis	
16	Asar, Ameshet, Apis	Osiris	Ba-Neb-Tattu—The Shoulders
17	Various twin Deities, Rekht, Merti, &c. [[Heru-Ra-Ha]]	The twin Merti	. . . .
18	Khephra	Hormakhu	. . . .
19	Ra-Hoor-Khuit, Pasht, Sekhet, Mau	Horus	As 6.
20	Isis [as Virgin]	Heru-pa-Kraath	. . . .
21	Amoun-Ra	Amoun-Ra	Apu-t—the Left Ear
22	Ma	Maat	. . . .
23	Tum, Ptah, Auramoth (as ▽), Asar (as Hanged Man), Hekar, Isis [[Hathor]]	Ⲓⲉ-ⲫⲣⲟⲧⲣⲉⲑ	As 24
24	Merti goddesses, Typhon, Apep, Khephra	Hammemit	Sekhet—the Belly and Back
25	Nephthys	Ⲇⲣⲱⲧⲉⲣⲓⲥ	. . . .
26	Khem (Set)	Set	As 10, for ע means Eye
27	Horus	Menθu	Khenti-Khas—the Right Nostril
28	Ahepi, Aroueris	Nuit	The Lords of Kereba—the Reins
29	Khephra (as Scarab in Tarot Trump)	Anubi	
30	Ra and many others	Ra	Hathor—the Right Eye
31	Thoum-Aesh-Neith, Mau, Kabeshunt, Horus, Tarpesheth.	Mau	[Serqet—the Teeth.] As 6.
32	Sebek, Mako	See Note *	Apu-t—the Right Ear
32 bis	Satem, Ahapshi, Nephthys, Ameshet	. . . .	אלים חיים—the Bones. As 16
31 bis	Asar	. . . .	. . . .

	XXII. Small selection of Hindu Deities.	XXIII.* The Forty Buddhist Meditations.	
0	AUM	Nothing and Neither P nor p' Space Consciousness	F F F
1	Parabrahm (or any other whom one wishes to please) [[Shiva, Brahma]]	Indifference	S
2	Shiva, Vishnu (as Buddha avatars), Akasa (as matter), Lingam	Joy	S
3	Bhavani (all forms of Sakti), Prana (as Force), Yoni	Compassion	S
4	Indra, Brahma	Friendliness	S
5	Vishnu, Varruna-Avatar	Death	R
6	Vishu-Hari-Krishna-Rama	Buddha	R
7	[[Bhavani, *etc.*]]	The Gods	R
8	Hanuman	Analysis into 4 Elements	A
9	Ganesha, Vishnu (Kurm Avatar)	Dhamma	R
10	Lakshmi, &c. [Kundalini]	Sangha The Body	R R
11	The Maruts [Vayu]	Wind	K
12	Hanuman, Vishnu (as Parasa-Rama)	Yellow	K
13	Chandra (as ☽)	Loathsomeness of Food	P
14	Lalita (sexual aspect of Sakti)	Dark Blue	K
15	Shiva	Bloody Corpse	I
16	Shiva (Sacred Bull)	Beaten and Scattered Corpse	I
17	Various twin and hybrid Deities	White	K
18	[[Krishna]]	Worm-eaten Corpse	I
19	Vishnu (Nara-Singh Avatar)	Gnawed by Wild Beasts Corpse	I
20	The Gopi girls, the Lord of Yoga	Bloated Corpse	I
21	Brahma, Indra	Liberality	R
22	Yama	Hacked in Pieces Corpse	I
23	Soma [Apas]	Water	K
24	Kundalini [[Yama]]	Skeleton Corpse	I
25	Vishnu (Horse-Avatar)	Limited Aperture	K
26	Lingam, Yoni	Putrid Corpse	I
27	[[Krishna]]	Blood-red	K
28	[[The Maruts]]	Purple Corpse	I
29	Vishnu (Matsya Avatar)	Conduct	R
30	Agni [Tejas], Yama [as God of Last Judgement]	Light	K
31	Surya (as ☉)	Fire	K
32	Brahma	Quiescence	R
32 bis	[Prithivi]	Earth	K
31 bis	[Akasa]	Breathing	R

TABLE I (*continued*) 9

	XXIV. Certain of the Hindu and Buddhist Results.	XXV.- XXXII.	XXXIII. Some Scandinavian Gods.	XXXIV. Some Greek Gods.
0	Nerodha-samapatti, Nirvikalpa-samadhi, Shiva darshana.		. . . . . .	Pan.
1	Unity with Brahma, Atma darshana		Wotan	Zeus, Iacchus
2	. . . .		Odin	Athena, Uranus [[Hermes]]
3	. . . .		Frigga	Cybele, Demeter, Rhea, Heré, [[Psyché, Kronos]]
4	. . . .		Wotan	Poseidon [[Zeus]]
5	. . . .		Thor	Ares, Hades
6	Vishvarupa-darshana		. . . . . .	Iacchus, Apollo, Adonis [[Dionysus, Bacchus]]
7	. . . .		Freya	Aphrodité, Niké
8	. . . .		Odin, Loki	Hermes
9	. . . .		. . . . . .	Zeus (as △), Diana of Epheus (as phallic stone [[and ♀]]) [[Eros]]
10	Vision of the "Higher Self," the various Dhyanas or Jhanas		. . . . . .	Persephone, [Adonis], Psyché
11	Vaya-Bhawana		Valkyries	Zeus
12	. . . .	We have insufficient knowledge of the attributions of Assyrian, Syrian, Mongolian, Tibetan, Mexican, Zend, South Sea, West African &c.	. . . . . .	Hermes
13	Vision of Chandra		. . . . . .	Artemis, Hekaté
14	Success in Bhaktioga		Freya	Aphrodité
15	. . . .		. . . . . .	Athena
16	Success in Hathayoga, Asana and Prana-yama		. . . . . .	[Heré]
17	. . . .		. . . . . .	Castor and Pollux, Apollo the Diviner [[Eros]]
18	. . . .		. . . . . .	Apollo the Charioteer
19	. . . .		. . . . . .	Demeter [borne by lions]
20	. . . .		. . . . . .	[Attis]
21	. . . .		. . . . . .	Zeus
22	. . . .		. . . . . .	Themis, Minos, Aeacus and Rhadamanthus
23	Apo-Bhawana		. . . . . .	Poseidon
24	. . . .		. . . . . .	Ares [[Apollo the Pythean, Thanatos]]
25	. . . .		. . . . . .	Apollo, Artemis (hunters)
26	. . . .		. . . . . .	Pan, Priapus [Erect Hermes and Bacchus]
27	. . . .		Tuisco	Ares, [[Athena]]
28	. . . .		. . . . . .	[Athena] Ganymede
29	. . . .		. . . . . .	Poseidon [[Hermes Psychopompos]]
30	Vision of Surya		. . . . . .	Helios, Apollo
31	Agni-Bhawana		. . . . . .	Hades
32	. . . .		. . . . . .	[Athena]
32 bis	Prithiva-Bhawana		. . . . . .	[Demeter] [[Gaia]]
31 bis	Vision of the Higher Self, Prana-yama.		. . . . . .	Iacchus

	XXXV. Some Roman Gods.	XXXVI. Selection of Christian Gods (10); Apostles (12); Evangelists (4) and Churches of Asia (7).	XXXVII. Hindu Legendary Demons.
0	. . . .	. . . .	. . . . .
1	Jupiter	God the 3 in 1	
2	Janus [[Mercury]]	God the Father, God who guides Parliament	
3	Juno, Cybele, Hecate, &c.	The Virgin Mary	
4	Jupiter [[Libitina]]	God the Rain-make (*vide* Prayer-book), God the Farmer's Friend	
5	Mars	Christ coming to Judge the World	
6	Apollo [[Bacchus, Aurora]]	God the Son (and Maker of fine Weather)	
7	Venus	Messiah, Lord of Hosts (*vide* Prayer-book, R. Kipling, &c.)	
8	Mercury	God the Holy Ghost (as Comforter and Inspirer of Scripture), God the Healer of Plagues	
9	Diana (as ☽) [[Terminus, Jupiter]]	God the Holy Ghost (as Incubus)	
10	Ceres	Ecclesia Xsti, the Virgin Mary	
11	Jupiter [[Juno, Æolus]]	Matthew	
12	Mercury	Sardis	
13	Diana	Laodicea	
14	Venus	Thyatira	
15	Mars, Minerva	[The Disciples are too indefinite]	
16	Venus [[Hymen]]	. . . .	
17	Castor and Pollux, [Janus] [[Hymen]]	. . . .	[Insufficient information.]
18	Mercury [[Lares and Penates]]	. . . .	
19	Venus (repressing the Fire of Vulcan)	. . . .	
20	[Attis], Ceres, Adonis [[Vesta, Flora]]	. . . .	
21	Jupiter, [Pluto]	Philadelphia	
22	Vulcan [[Venus, Nemesis]]	. . . .	
23	Neptune [[Rhea]]	John, Jesus as Hanged Man	
24	Mars [[Mors]]	. . . .	
25	Diana (as Archer) [[Iris]]	. . . .	
26	Pan, Vesta, Bacchus	. . . .	
27	Mars	Pergamos	
28	Juno [[Æolus]]	. . . .	
29	Neptune	. . . .	
30	Apollo [[Ops]]	Smyrna	
31	Vulcan, Pluto	Mark	
32	Saturn [[Terminus, Astræa]]	Ephesus	
32 bis	Ceres	Luke	
31 bis	[Liber] [[Bacchus]]	The Holy Ghost	

TABLE I (continued)　　　　　　　　II

	XXXVIII.* Animals, Real and Imaginary.	XXXIX.* Plants, Real and Imaginary.
0	[[Dragon]]	[[Lotus, Rose]]
1	God [[Swan, Hawk]]	Almond in Flower [[Banyan]]
2	Man	Amaranth [[Mistletoe, Bo or Pipal Tree]]
3	Woman [[Bee]]	Cypress, Opium Poppy [[Lotus, Lily, Ivy]]
4	Unicorn	Olive, Shamrock [[Opium Poppy]]
5	Basilisk	Oak, Nux Vomica, Nettle [[Hickory]]
6	Phœnix, Lion, Child [[Spider, Pelican]]	Acacia, Bay, Laurel, Vine [[Oak, Gorse, Ash, Aswata]]
7	Iynx [[Raven, all carrion birds]]	Rose [[Laurel]]
8	Hermaphrodite, Jackal [[Twin serpents, Monoceros de Astris]]	Moly, Anhalonium Lewinii
9	Elephant [[Tortoise, Toad]]	[Banyan], Mandrake, Damiana [[Ginseng, Yohimba]]
10	Sphinx	Willow, Lily, Ivy [[Pomegranate, all cereals]]
11	Eagle, Man (Cherub of △) [[Ox]]	Aspen
12	Swallow, Ibis, Ape [[Twin Serpents, fish, hybrids]]	Vervain, Herb Mercury, Major-lane, Palm [[Lime or Linden]]
13	Dog [[Stork, Camel]]	Almond, Mugwort, Hazel (as ☽), Moonwort, Ranunculus [[Alder, Pomegranate]]
14	Sparrow, Dove [[Swan, Sow, birds generally]]	Myrtle, Rose, Clover [[Fig, Peach, Apple]]
15	Ram, Owl	Tiger Lily, Geranium [[Olive]]
16	Bull (Cherub of ▽) [[all beasts of Burden]]	Mallow [[all giant trees]]
17	Magpie, hybrids [[Parrot, Zebra, Penguin]]	Hybrids, Orchids
18	Crab, Turtle, Sphinx [[Whale, all beasts of Transport]]	Lotus
19	Lion (Cherub of △) [[Cat, Tiger, Serpent, Woman]]	Sunflower
20	Virgin, Anchorite, any solitary person or animal [[Rhinoceros]]	Snowdrop, Lily, Narcissus [[Mistletoe]]
21	Eagle [[Praying Mantis]]	Hyssop, Oak, Poplar, Fig [[Arnica, Cedar]]
22	Elephant [[Spider]]	Aloe
23	Eagle-Snake-Scorpion (Cherub of ▽)	Lotus, all Water Plants
24	Scorpio, Beetle, Crayfish or Lobster, Wolf [[all Reptiles, Shark, Crablouse]]	Cactus [[Nettle, all poisonous plants]]
25	Centaur, Horse, Hippogriff, Dog	Rush
26	Goat, Ass [[Oyster]]	Indian Hemp, Orchis Root, Thistle [[Yohimba]]
27	Horse, Bear, Wolf [[Boar]]	Absinthe, Rue
28	Man or Eagle (Cherub of △), Peacock	[Olive], Cocoanut
29	Fish, Dolphin [[Beetle, Dog, Jackal]]	Unicellular Organisms, Opium [[Mangrove]]
30	Lion, Sparrowhawk [[Leopard]]	Sunflower, Laural, Heliotrop [[Nut, Galangal]]
31	Lion (Cherub of △)	Red Poppy, Hibiscus, Nettle [[all scarlet flowers]]
32	Crocodile	Ash, Cypress, Hellebore, Yew, Nightshade [[Elm]]
32 bis	Bull (Cherub of ▽)	Oak, Ivy [[Cereals]]
31 bis	Sphinx (if sworded and crowned)	Almond in Flower

	XL.* Precious Stones.	XLI. Magical Weapons.	CLXXXVII. Magical Formulæ (see Col. XLI)
0	[[Star Sapphire, Black Diamond]]	[[No attribution possible]]	LASTAL. M . . . . M
1	Diamond	Swastika or Fylfot Cross, Crown [[The Lamp]]	. . . .
2	Star Ruby, Turquoise	Lingam, the Inner Robe of Glory [[The Word]]	VIAOV
3	Star Sapphire, Pearl	Yoni, the Outer Robe of Concealment [[The Cup, the Shining Star]]	BABALON. VITRIOL
4	Amethyst, Sapphire [[Lapis Lazuli]]	The Wand, Sceptre, or Crook	IHVH
5	Ruby	The Sword, Spear, Scourge, or Chain	AGLA. ALHIM
6	Topaz, Yellow Diamond	The Lamen or Rosy Cross	ABRAHADABRA. IAO: INRI
7	Emerald	The Lamp and Girdle	ARARITA
8	Opal, especially Fire Opal	The Names and Versicles and Apron	. . . .
9	Quartz	The Perfumes and Sandals [[The Altar]]	ALIM
10	Rock Crystal	The Magical Circle and Triangle	VITRIOL
11	Topaz	The Dagger or Fan	. . . .
12	Opal, Agate	The Wand or Caduceus	. . . .
13	Moonstone, Pearl, Crystal	Bow and Arrow	ALIM
14	Emerald, Turquoise	The Girdle	ΑΓΑΠΗ
15	Ruby	The Horns, Energy, the Burin	. . . .
16	Topaz	The Labour of Preparation [[The Throne and Altar]]	. . . .
17	Alexandrite, Tourmaline, Iceland Spar	The Tripod	. . . .
18	Amber	The Furnace [[The Cup or Holy Graal]]	ABRAHADABRA
19	Cat's Eye	The Discipline (Preliminary) [[Phœnix Wand]]	ΤΟ ΜΕΓΑ ΘΗΡΙΟΝ
20	Peridot	The Lamp and Wand (Virile Force reserved), the Bread [[Lotus Wand]]	. . . .
21	Amethyst, Lapis Lazuli	The Sceptre	. . . .
22	Emerald	The Cross of Equilibrium	. . . .
23	Beryl or Aquamarine	The Cup and Cross of Suffering, the Wine [[Water of Lustration]]	. . . .
24	Snakestone [[Greenish Turquoise]]	The Pain of the Obligation [[The Oath]]	AUMGN
25	Jacinth	The Arrow (swift and straight application of force)	ON
26	Black Diamond	The Secret Force, Lamp	ON
27	Ruby, any red stone	The Sword	. . . .
28	Artificial Glass [[Chalcedony]]	The Censer or Aspergillus	. . . .
29	Pearl	The Twilight of the Place and Magic Mirror	. . . .
30	Crysolith	The Lamen or Bow and Arrow	IAO : INRI
31	Fire Opal	The Wand or Lamp, Pyramid of △ [[The Thurible]]	. . . .
32	Onyx	A Sickle	. . . .
32 bis	Salt	The Pantacle or [[Bread and]] Salt	. . . .
31 bis	Black Diamond	[[The Winged Egg]]	. . . .

TABLE I (*continued*) 13

	XLII.* Perfumes.	XLIII.* Vegetable Drugs.	XLIV.* Mineral Drugs.
0	[[No attribution possible]]	. . . .	Carbon
1	Ambergris	Elixir Vitæ	Aur. Pot.
2	Musk	Hashish [[Cocaine]]	Phosphorus
3	Myrrh, Civet	Belladonna, Soma	Silver
4	Cedar	Opium	. . . .
5	Tobacco	Nux Vomica, Nettle [[Cocaine, Atropine]]	Iron, Sulphur
6	Olibanum	Stramonium, Alcohol, Digitalis, Coffee	. . . .
7	Benzoin, Rose, Red Sandal	Damiana, Cannabis Indica [[Anhalonium]]	Arsenic
8	Storax	Anhalonium Lewinii [[Cannabis Indica]]	Mercury
9	Jasmine, Jinseng, all Odoriferous Roots	Orchid Root	Lead
10	Dittany of Crete	Corn	Mag. Sulph.
11	Galbanum	Peppermint	. . . .
12	Mastic, White Sandal, [[Nutmeg]], Mace, Storax, all Fugitive Odours.	All cerebral excitants	Mercury
13	Menstrual Blood, Camphor, Aloes, all Sweet Virginal Odours	Jupiter, Pennyroyal, & all emmenogogues	. . . .
14	Sandalwood, Myrtle, all Soft Voluptuous Odours	All aphrodisiacs	. . . .
15	Dragon's Blood	All cerebral excitants	. . . .
16	Storax	Sugar	. . . .
17	Wormwood	Ergot and ecbolics	. . . .
18	Onycha	Watercress	. . . .
19	Olibanum	All carminatives and tonics	. . . .
20	Narcissus	All anaphrodisiacs	. . . .
21	Saffron, all Generous Odours	Cocaine	. . . .
22	Galbanum	Tobacco	. . . .
23	Onycha, Myrrh	Caseara, all purges	Sulphates
24	Siamese Benzoin, Opoponax	. . . .	. . . .
25	Lign-aloes	. . . .	. . . .
26	Musk, Civet (also ♄ian Perfumes)	Orchis [Satyrion]	. . . .
27	Pepper, Dragon's Blood, all Hot Pungent Odours	. . . .	. . . .
28	Galbanum	All diuretics	. . . .
29	Ambergris [[Menstrual Fluid]]	All narcotics	. . . .
30	Olibanum, Cinnamon, all Glorious Odours	Alcohol	. . . .
31	Olibanum, all Fiery Odours	. . . .	Nitrates
32	Assafœtida, Scammony, Indigo, Sulphur (all Evil Odours)	. . . .	Lead
32 bis	Storax, all Dull and Heavy Odours	. . . .	Bismuth
31 bis	[[No attribution possible]]	Stramonium	Carbon

	XLV. Magical Powers [Western Mysticism].	XLVI. System of Taoism.
0	The Supreme Attainment [[Vision of No Difference]]	The Tao or Great Extreme of the Yi King.
1	Union with God	Shang Ti (also the Tao)
2	The Vision of God face to face [[Vision of Antinomies]]	The Yang and Khien
3	The Vision of Sorrow [[Vision of Wonder]]	Kwan-se-on, The Yin and Khwan.
4	The Vision of Love	. . . .
5	The Vision of Power	. . . .
6	The Vision of the Harmony of Things (also the Mysteries of the Crucifixion), [[Beatific Vision]]	Li
7	The Vision of Beauty Triumphant	. . . .
8	The Vision of Splendour [Ezekiel]	. . . .
9	The Vision of the Machinery of the Universe	. . . .
10	The Vision of the Holy Guardian Angel or of Adonai.	Khan
11	Divination	Sun
12	Miracles of Healing, Gift of Tongues, Knowledge of Sciences	Sun
13	The White Tincture, Clairvoyance, Divination by Dreams	Kan and Khwan
14	Love-philtres	Tui
15	Power of Consecrating Things	. . . .
16	The Secret of Physical Strength	. . . .
17	Power of being in two or more places at one time, and of Prophecy	. . . .
18	Power of Casting Enchantments	. . . .
19	Power of Training Wild Beasts	. . . .
20	Invisibility, Parthenogenesis, Initiation (?)	. . . .
21	Power of Acquiring Political and other Ascendency.	Li
22	Works of Justice and Equilibrium	. . . .
23	The Great Work, Talismans, Crystal-gazing, & c.	Tui
24	Necromancy	. . . .
25	Transmutations [[Vision of Universal Peacock]]	. . . .
26	The Witches' Sabbath so-called, the Evil Eye	. . . .
27	Works of Wrath and Vengeance	Kăn
28	Astrology	. . . .
29	Bewitchments, Casting Illusions	. . . .
30	The Red Tincture, Power of Acquiring Wealth	Li and Khien
31	Evocation, Pyromancy	Kăn
32	Works of Malediction and Death	Khăn
32 bis	Alchemy, Geomancy, Making of Pantacles, [[Travels on the Astral Plane]]	Kăn
31 bis	Invisibility, Transformations, Vision of the Genius	. . . .

TABLE I (*continued*)   **15**

	XLVII. Kings and Princes of the Jinn.	XLVIII. Figures related to Pure Number.	XLIX.* Lineal Figures of the Planets, &c., and Geomany.
0	. . . .	. . . .	The Circle
1	. . . .	. . . .	The Point
2	. . . .	The Cross	The Line, also the Cross
3	. . . .	The Triangle	The Plane, also the Diamond, Oval, Circle, and other Yoni Symbols
4	[column	Tetrahedron or Pyramid, Cross	The Solid Figure
5	left	The Rose	The Tesseract
6	blank	Calvary Cross, Truncated Pyramid, Cube.	⎫ Sephirothic Geomantic Figures
7	due	A Rose (7 x 7), Candlestick	⎪ follow the Planets. Caput* and
8	to	. . . .	⎪ Cauda Draconis* are the Nodes of
9	transcriber's	. . . .	⎬ the Moon, nearly = Neptune and
10	complete	Altar (Double Cube), Calvary Cross	⎪ Herschel respectively. They
11	ignorance	. . . .	Those of △y Triplicity
12	of	Calvary Cross	Octagram
13	Arabic.	Greek Cross (Plane), Table of Shew-bread	Enneagram
14	May	. . . .	Heptagram
15	be	. . . .	Puer *
16	restored	. . . .	Amissio *
17	at	Swastika	Albus *
18	some	. . . .	Populus and Via *
19	point,	. . . .	Fortuna Major and Fortuna Minor *
20	but	. . . .	Conjunctio *
21	then	. . . .	Square and Rhombus
22	again	Greek Cross Solid, the Rose (3 + 7 + 12)	Puella
23	maybe	. . . .	Those of ▽y Triplicity
24	not;	. . . .	Rubeus *
25	in	The Rose (5 x 5)	Acquisitio *
26	any	Calvary Cross of 10, Solid	Carcer *
27	case	. . . .	Pentagram
28	don't	. . . .	Tristitia *
29	hold	. . . .	Laetitia *
30	your	. . . .	Hexagram
31	breath	. . . .	Those of △y Triplicity
32	folks.]	. . . .	Triangle
32 bis	. . . .	. . . .	Those of ▽y Triplicity
31 bis	. . . .	. . . .	. . . .

	L.* Transcendental Morality. [10 Virtues (1-10), 7 Sins (Planets), 4 Magick Powers (Elements).]	LI. The Coptic Alphabet.		Names of Coptic letters.	Numeration of Col. LI.	English equivalent of Col. LI.
0	. . . .	. . .		. . .	. . . . .	. . .
1	Pyrrho-Zoroastrianusm (Accom- plishment of Great Work)	Ⲉ	ⲉ	Sou	6	St
2	Devotion	Ⲋ	ⲋ	Gima	. . . . . .	Sz
3	Silence	Ⲑ	ⲑ	Ti	. . . . . .	Tt
4	Obedience	Ⲏ	ⲏ	Heta	8	Æ
5	Energy	Ⲫ	ⲫ	Phi	500	Ph
6	Devotion to Great Work	Ⲱ	ⲱ	Ö	800	ōō (long O)
7	Unselfishness	Ⲉ	ⲉ	Ei	5	E
8	Truthfulness	Ⳝ	ⳝ	Fai	90	f, v
9	Independence	Ⲭ	ⲭ	Janja	. . . .	J
10	Scepticism	Ⲥ	ⲥ	Sémma	200	S
11	Noscere	Ⲁ	ⲁ	Alpha	1	A
12	Falsehood, Dishonesty [Envy]	Ⲃ	ⲃ	Beta	2	B
13	Contentment [Idleness]	Ⲅ	ⲅ	Gamma	3	G
14	Unchastity [Lust]	Ⲇ	ⲇ	Dalda	4	D
15	. . . .	Ⲉ	ⲉ	Hori	. . . . . .	H
16	. . . .	Ⲩ	ⲩ	He	400	U
17	. . . .	Ⲍ	ⲍ	Zéta	7	Z
18	. . . .	Ⳃ	ⳃ	Khei	. . . . . .	Ch
19	. . . .	Ⲑ	ⲑ	Théta	9	Th
20	. . . .	Ⲓ	ⲓ	Yota	10	I, y, ee
21	Bigotry, Hypocrisy [Gluttony]	Ⲕ	ⲕ	Kappa	20	K
22	. . . .	Ⲗ	ⲗ	Lauda	30	L
23	Audere	Ⲙ	ⲙ	Mé	40	M
24	. . . .	Ⲛ	ⲛ	Nr	50	N
25	. . . .	Ⲝ	ⲝ	Ksi	60	X
26	. . . .	Ⲟ	ⲟ	Ow	70	O
27	Cruelty [Wrath]	Ⲡ	ⲡ	Pi	80	P
28	. . . .	Ⲯ	ⲯ	Psi	700	Ps
29	. . . .	Ⲭ	ⲭ	Khi	600	Q
30	[Pride]	Ⲣ	ⲣ	Ro	100	R
31	Velle	Ⲩ	ⲯ	Shai	900	Sh
32	Envy [Avarice]	Ⲧ	ⲧ	Taw	300	T
32 bis	Tacere	. . . .		. . . . .	. . .	
31 bis	. . . .	. . . .		. . . . .	. . .	. . . . .

TABLE I (*continued*)   17

	LII. The Arabic Alphabet.	CLXXXIV. Numeration of Arabic Alphabet	LIII. The Greek Alphabet.	CLXXXV. Numeration of Greek Alphabet	CLXXXVI. Diseases (Typical).
0	. . . . .	. . . .	. . . . . .	. . . . .	. . . .
1	Three Lost	. . . .	. . . . . .	31	Death
2	Fathers.	. . . .	[σ]	200	Insanity
3		. . . .	. . . . . .	. . . . . .	Dementia (Amnesia)
4	ث thä	500	[ε]	. . . . . .	Dropsy
5	خ khā	600	[φ]	500	Fever
6	د dal	700	ω	800	Heart Lesions
7	ض ḍād	800	[ε]	. . . . . .	Skin Troubles
8	ظ ẓa	900	. . . .	. . . . . .	Nerve Troubles
9	غ ghain	1000	χ	600	Impotence
10	غ ghain	. . . .	ꝫ	900	Sterility
11	ا alif	1	a	1	Fluxes
12	ب bä	2	β	2	Ataxia
13	ج jim	3	γ	3	Menstrual Disorders
14	د dāl	4	δ	4	Syphilis, Gonorrhoea
15	ه hā	5	ε	5	Apoplex
16	و wāw	6	ϝ	6	Indigestion
17	ز zā	7	ζ	7	Phthysis, Pneumonia
18	ح ḥā	8	η	8	Rheumatism
19	ط ṭā	9	θ	9	Syncope, etc. Heart
20	ي yā	10	ι	10	Spinal weakness, Paralysis
21	ك käf	20	κ	20	Gout
22	ل läm	30	λ	30	Kidney disorders
23	م mīm	40	μ	40	Chill
24	ن nūn	50	ν	50	Cancer
25	س sīn	60	ξ [σ]	60	Apoplexy, Thrombosis
26	ع äyn	70	o	70	Arthritis
27	ف fa	80	π	80	Inflammation
28	ص ṣād	90	ψ	700	Cystitis
29	ق qäf	100	ϙ	90	Gout
30	ر rā	200	ρ	100	Repletion
31	ش shīn	300	ꝫ	900	Fever
32	ت tä	400	τ	300	Arterio Sclerosis
32 bis	. . . . . .	. . . . . .	. . . . .	υ	400	Sluggishness
31 bis	. . . . . .	. . . . . .	. . . . .	. . . . . .	Death (full Insanity)

	LIV. The Letters of the Name	LV. The Elements and Senses.	LVI. The Four Rivers.	LVII.* The Four Quarters.	LVIII. Supereme Elemental Kings.
11	ו	△ Air, Smell	חדקל Hiddekel	(E) מזרח Mezrach	Tahoeloj
23	ח	▽ Water, Taste	גחון Gihon	(W) מערב Maareb	Thahebyobeaatan
31	י	△ Fire, Sight	פישון Pison	(S) דרום Darom	Ohooohatan
32 bis	ה	▽ Earth, Touch	פרת Phrath	(N) צפון Tzaphon	Thahaaothahe
31 bis	ש	✳ Spirit, Hearing	. . . .	. . . .	. . . .

	LIX. Archangels of the Quarters.	LX. The Rulers of the Elements	LXI. Angels of the elements.	LXII. Kings of the Elemental Spirits.
11	רפאל Raphael	אריאל Ariel	חסן Chassan	Paralda
23	גבריאל Gabriel	תרשים Tharsis	תליהד Taliahad	Niksa
31	מיכאל Michael	שרף Seraph	אראל Aral	Djin
32 bis	אוריאל Auriel	כרוב Kerub	פורלאך Phorlakh	Ghob
31 bis	. . . .	. . . .	. . . .	. . . .

	LXIII. The Four Worlds.	LXIV. Secret Names of the Four Words.	LXV. Secret Numbers corresponding.	LXVI. Spelling of Tetragrammaton in the Four Worlds.
11	יצירה Yetrizah, Formative World	מה Mah	45	יוד הא ואו הא
23	בריאה Briah, Creative World	סג Seg	63	יוד הא ואו הא
31	צילות Atziluth, Archetypal World א	עב Aub	72	יוד הי ויו הי
32 bis	עשיה Assiah, Material World	בן Ben	52	יוד הה וו הה
31 bis	. . . .	. . . .	. . . .	

	LXVII. The Parts of the Soul.	LXVIII. The Demon Kings.	LXIX.* The Alchemical Elements.	LXX. Attribution of Pentagram.
11	רוח Ruach	Oriens	☿	Left Upper Point
23	נשמה Neshamah	Ariton	⊖	Right Upper Point
31	חיה Chiah	Paimon	🜍	Right Lower Point
32 bis	נפש Nephesh	Amaimon	⊖	Left Lower Point
31 bis	יחידה Yechidah	. . . .	. . . .	Topmost Point

TABLE II *(continued)*   19

	LXXI. The Court Cards of the Tarot, with the Spheres of their Celestial Dominion—Wands.	LXXII. The Court Cards of the Tarot, with the Spheres of their Celestial Dominion—Cups.
11	The Prince of the Chariot of Fire. Rules 20° ♋ to 20° ♍, including most of Leo Minor.	The Prince of the Chariot of the Waters. 20° ♎ to 20° ♏
23	The Queen of the Thrones of Flame. 20° ♓ to 20° ♈, including part of Andromeda.	The Queen of the Thrones of the Waters. 20° ♊ to 20° ♋
31	The Lord of the Flame and the Lightning. The King of the Spirits of Fire. Rules 20° ♏ to 20° ♐, including part of Hercules.	The Lord of the Waves and the Waters. The King of the Hosts of the Sea. 20° ♒ to 20° ♓, including most of Pegasus.
32 bis	The Princess of the Shining Flame. The Rose of the Palace of Fire. Rules one Quadrant of Heavens round N. Pole.	The Princess of the Waters. The Rose of the Palace of the Floods. Rules another Quadrant
31 bis	The Root of the Powers of Fire (Ace)	The Root of the Powers of Water.

	LXXIII. The Court Cards of the Tarot, with the Spheres of their Celestial Dominion—Swords.	LXXIV. The Court Cards of the Tarot, with the Spheres of their Celestial Dominion—Pantacles.
11	The Prince of the Chariot of Air. 20° ♑ to 20° ♒	The Prince of the Chariot of Earth. 20° ♈ to 20° ♉
23	The Queen of the Thrones of Air. 20° ♍ to 20° ♎	The Queen of the Thrones of the Earth. 20° ♐ to 20° ♑
31	The Lord of the Winds and the Breezes. The King of the Spirits of Air. 20° ♉ to 20° ♊	The Lord of the Wide and Fertile Land. The King of the Spirits of Earth. 20° ♌ to 20° ♍
32 bis	The Princess of the Rushing Winds. The Lotus of the Palace of Air. Rules a 3rd Quadrant.	The Princess of the Echoing Hills. The Lotus of the Palace of the Earth. Rules a 4th Quadrant of the Heavens about Kether.
31 bis	The Root of the Powers of Air	The Root of the Powers of Water.

	LXXV. The Five Elements (Tatwas).	LXXVI. The Five Skandhas.	English of Col. LXXVI.	CLXXXVIII. The Body.
11	Vayu—the Blue Circle	*sankhāra*	Mental-formation ('tendency')	Breath
23	Apas—the Silver Crescent	*vedanā*	Feeling	Chyle, Lymph
31	Agni or Tejas—the Red Triangle	*sañña*	Perception	Blood
32 bis	Prithivi—the Yellow Square	*rūpa*	Corporeality	Solid structures, tissues
31 bis	Akasa—the Black Egg	*viññāṇam*	Consciousness	Semen, Marrow

	CXCI. The Four Noble Truths (Buddhism)	CLXXXIX. CXC. Bodily Functions.	
11	Sorrow's Cause	Speaking	Though
23	Sorrow's Ceasing	Holding	Nutrition
31	Noble Eight-fold Path	Moving	Moving
32 bis	Sorrow	Excreting	Matter
31 bis	. . . .	Generating	Magick

	LXXVII. The Planets and their Numbers.		LXXVIII. Intelligences of the Planets.	CXCIV (transliteration)
12	☿	8	תיריאל (260)	Tiriel
13	☽	9	מלכא בתרשישים ועד ברוח שחקים (3321)	Malkah Be Tarshishim va A'ad Be Ruah Shehaqim.
14	♀	7	חניאל (49)	Hagiel
21	♃	4	יופיל (136)	Yophiel
27	♂	5	גראפיאל (325)	Graphiel
30	☉	6	נכיאל (111)	Nakhiel
32	♄	3	אגיאל (45)	Agiel

	LXXIX. Spirits of the Planets.*	CXCIII. (transliteration)	LXXX. Olympic Planetary Spirits.	LXXXI. Metals.	LXXXII. The Noble Eightfold Path.
12	תפתרתרת (2080)	Taphthartharath	Ophiel	Mercury	Samma Vaca
13	חשמודאי (369)	Chasmodai	Phul	Silver	Samma Sankappo
14	קדמאל (175)	Qedemel	Hagith	Copper	Samma Kammanto
21	הסמאל (136)	Hismael	Bethor	Tin	Samma Ajivo
27	ברצבאל (325)	Bartzabel	Phaleg	Iron	Samma Vayamo
30	סורת (666)	Sorath	Och	Gold	Samma Samadhi
32	זאזל (45)	Zazel	Arathron	Lead	Samma Sati and Samaditthi

	CXCII. English of Col. LXXXII	LXXXIII. The Attribution of the Hexagram.
12	Right Speech	Left Lower Point
13	Right Aspiration	Bottom Point
14	Right Conduct	Right Lower Point
21	Right Discipline	Right Upper Point
27	Right Energy	Left Lower Point
30	Right Rapture	Centre Point
32	Right Recollection (in both senses of the word). Right View-Point.	Top Point

TABLE IV 21

	LXXXIV. Divine Names of Briah.	LXXXV. Angels of Briah.	LXXXVI. Choirs of Angels in Briah.	LXXXVII. Palaces of Briah.
1	} אל {	יהואל Yehuel	שרפים Seraphim	} היכל קדוש קדשים Hekel Qadosh Qadeshim
2		רפאל Raphael	אופנים Auphanim	
3		כרוביאל Kerubiel	כרובים Kerubim	
4	(sic) מצפצ	צדקיאל Tzadqiel	שיננים Shinanim	היכל אהבה H. Ahbah
5	יהוד	תרשיש Tharshish	תרשישים Tharshishim	היכל זכות H. Zakoth
6	יהוה	מתתרון * Metatron	חשמלים Chashmalim	היכל רצון H. Ratzon
7	אלהים	וסיאל Usiel	מלכים Malakim	היכל עצם שמים H. Etzem Shamaim
8	מצפץ	חסניאל Hisniel	בני אלהים Beni Elohim	היכל גונה H. Gonah
9	} אל־אדני {	יהואל * Yehuel	ישים Ishim	} ח. לבנת הספיר H. Lebanath ha-Saphir
10		מיכאל Michael	אראלים Aralim	

	LXXXVIII. Translation of Col. LXXXVII.	LXXXIX.* The Revolutions of אהיה in Briah	XC. The 42-fold Name which revolves in the Palaces of Yetzirah.	XCI. The Saints or Adepts of the Hebrews
1	} Palace of the Holy of Holies {	אהיה	אב	Messias filius David
2		אהיי	גי	Mosheh
3		איהה	טצ	Enoch
4	P. of Love	חהיא	קרעשטן	Abraham
5	P. of Merit	חהאי	בגריכש	Jacob
6	P. of Benevolence	האהי	במרצתג	Elijah
7	P. of the Substance of Heaven	האיה	חקממנע	Mosheh
8	P. of Serenity	היאה	יגלפזק	Aaron
9	} Palace of Crystalline Whiteness {	יאהה	שקי	Joseph (Justus)
10		יההא / יהאה / אל שרי	עית	David, Elisha

	XCII. The Angelic Functions in the World of Yetzirah.	XCIII. The Heavens of Assiah.	XCIV. English of Palaces (Col. XCIII).
1			
2	} Above it stood the seraphim: six wings	ערבות Araboth	Plain
3			
4	Six wings	מכון Makhon	Emplacement
5	One : with two	מעון Maon	Residence
6	he covered his faces: and with two he covered	זבול Zebul	Dwelling
7	his feet and	שחקים Shechaqim	Clouds
8	with two he was flying.	רקיע Raquia	Firmament
9	{ And one cried to the other and said: Holy, holy, holy, Lord of Hosts, the whole earth is full of his glory.	תבל וילון שמים Tebel Vilon Shamaim	Veil of the vault of heaven
10			

	XCV. Contents of Col. XCIV.	XCVI.* The Revolutions of יהוה in Yetzirah.	XCVII. Parts of the Soul.	XCVIII. English of Col. XCVII..
1	⎫	יהוה	יחידה Yechidah	The Self
2	⎬ Blessings, all good things	יההו	חיה Chiah	The Life Force
3	⎭	יוהה	נשמה Neshamah	The Intuition
4	Snow, rain, spirit of life, blessings	הויה		
5	Angels singing in Divine Presence	ההוי		
6	Altar, Mikhael offering souls of just	ההיו		
7	Millstones where manna for just is ground for future	היהו	רוח Ruach	The Intellect
8	Sol, Luna, planets, stars, and 10 spheres	היהי		
9	⎫	והיה		
10	⎬ Has no use. Follow 390 heavens, 18,000 worlds, Earth, Eden and Hell.	ויהה / והחי / אל יהוה	נפש Nephesh	The Animal Soul, which perceives and feeds.

	XCIX.* Archangels of Assiah.	C.* Angels of Assiah.	CI. English of Col. C.	CII.* The Revolutions of Adonai in Assiah.
1	מטטרון Metatron	חיות הקדש Chaioth ha-Qadosh	Holy living creatures	אדני
2	רציאל Ratziel	אופנים Auphanim	Wheels	אדינ
3	צפקיאל Tzaphkiel	אראלים Aralim	Active ones, thrones	אניד
4	צדקיאל Tzadkiel	חשמלים Chashmalim	Brilliant ones	אינד
5	כמאל Kamael	שרפים Seraphim	Fiery serpents	אדרנ
6	רפאל Raphael	מלכים Malakim	Kings	דניא
7	האניאל Haniel	אלהים Elohim	Gods	דנאי
8	מיכאל Mikael	בני אלהים Beni Elohim	Sons of God	דינא
9	גבריאל Gabriel	כרובים Kerubim	Angels of elements	ריאנ
10	סנדלפון Sandalphon (מטטרון) (Metatron)	אשים Ashim	Flames	דאני / ראינ / אל אדני

	CIII.* The Ten Divisions of the Body of God.	CIV. The Ten Earths in Seven Palaces.	CV. English of Col. CIV.
1	Skull		
2	Right brain	ארץ Aretz	Earth (dry)
3	Left brain		
4	Right arm	אדמה Adamah	Red earth
5	Left arm	גיא Gia	Undulating ground
6	The whole body from the throat to the holy member	נשיה Neshiah	Pasture
7	Right left	ציה Tziah	Sandy earth
8	Left leg	ארקא Arqa	Earth
9	Sign of the holy covenant	תבל Tebhel	Wet earth
10	Crown which is in Yesod	חלד Cheled	

TABLE IV (*continued*) 23

	CVI. * The Ten Hells in Seven Palaces.	CVII. Translation of Hells.	CVIII.* Some Princes of the Qliphoth.	CIX.* The Kings of Edom.
1	שאול Sheol	Grave	Satan and Moloch	. . . .
2			כמאל *	. . . .
3			אשת זנונים	. . . .
4	אבדון Abaddon	Perdition	Lucifuge	בצרה יובב of Jobab of Bozrah
5	באר שחת Bar Shachath	Clay of Death	אשתרום	חשם תימני Husham of Temani
6	טיטהיון Titahion	Pit of Destruction	Belphegor חיוא	הדד עית Hadad of Avith
7	שעירמות Shaarimoth	Gates of Death	אשמדאי	שנמלה משרקה Samlah of Masrekah
8	אלמות Tzelmoth	Shadow of Death	Adramelek בליאל	שאול רהבית Saul of Reheboth
9	גיהנם Gehinnom	Hell	לילית	בעל חנן Baal-Hannan
10			נעמה	הדר פעו Hadar of Pau

	CIX. (*continued*)* The Dukes of Edom.	CX. Elements and Quarters (Sepher Yetzirah).	CXI. Sephirothic Colours (Dr. Jellinek).
1	. . . .	רוח אלהים חיים	Concealed Light
2	. . . .	Air	Sky Blue
3	. . . .	Water and Earth	Yellow
4	אהליבמה Aholibamah	Fire	White
5	אלה Elah	Height	Red
6	פינן Pinon	Depth	White-red
7	קנז Kenaz	East	Whitish-red
8	תימן Teman	West	Reddish-white
9	מבצר and מגדיאל Mibzar and Magdiel	South	White-red-whitsh-red-reddish-white
10	עירם Eram	North	The Light reflecting all colours

	CXII. Alchemical Tree of Life (i.).	CXIII. Alchemical Metals (ii.).	CXIV. Passwords of the Grades.	CXV.* Officers in a Masonic Lodge.	CXVI. Egyptian Attribution of Parts of the Soul.
0	. . . .	. . . .	. . . .	. . . .	Hammemit
1	☿	Metallic Radix.	Silence *		Kha, or Yekh
2	♃	♄	(3) אב	Past Master	Khai, or Ka
3	♁	♂	(6) רב		Ba, or Baie
4	♆	♆	(10) אט	Worshipful Master	
5	☉	☉	(15) יה	Senior Warden	
6	♂	♂	(21) אהיה	Junion Warden	Aib
7	♃	♀	(28) כח	Senior Deacon	
8	♀	♀	(36) אלה	Junior Deacon	
9	☿	☿	(45) מה	Inner Guard	Hati
10	Mercurius Philosophorum	Medicina Metallorum	(55) נה	Tyler and Candidate	Kheibt, Khat, Tet, Sahu

	CXVII. The Soul (Hindu).	CXVIII. The Chakkras or Centres of Prana (Hinduism).	CXIX. The Ten Fetters (Buddhism).	English of Col. CXIX.
1	Atma	Sahasrara (above Head)	Aruparga	Desire for immaterial immortality
2	Buddhi	Ajna (Pineal Gland)	Vikkikika	Sceptical doubt.
3	Higher Manas	Visuddhi (Larynx)	Rupraga	Desire for bodily immortality
4	} Lower Manas	Anahata (heart)	{ Silabata Paramesa	Clinging to rules and ritual
5			Patigha	Hatred.
6			Udakkha	Restlessness.
7	Kama	Manipura (Solar Plexus)	Mano	Pride.
8	Prana	Svadistthana (Navel)	Sakkya-ditti	Belief in a personality or "soul"
9	Linga Sharira	Muladhara (Lingam and Anus)	Kama	Bodily desire
10	Sthula Sharira		Avigga	Ignorance.

	CXX. Magical Images of the Sephiroth.	CXXI.* The Grades of the Order.		CXXII. The Ten Plagues of Egypt.
0	. . . .	$0^\square = 0^\circ$		. . . .
1	Ancient bearded king seen in profile	$10^\circ = 1^\square$ Ipsissimus	} 3rd Order	{ Death of First-born
2	Almost any male image shows some aspect of Chokmah.	$9^\circ = 2^\square$ Magus		Locusts
3	Almost any female image shows some aspect of Binah	$8^\circ = 3^\square$ Magister Templi		Darkness
4	A mighty crowned and enthroned king	$7^\circ = 4^\square$ Adeptus Exemptus	} 2nd Order	{ Hail and Fire
5	A mighty warrior in his chariot, armed and crowned	$6^\circ = 5^\square$ Adeptus Major		Boils
6	A majestic king, a child, a crucified god	$5^\circ = 6^\square$ Adeptus Minor		Murrain
7	A beautiful naked woman	$4^\circ = 7^\square$ Philosophus	} 1st Order	{ Flies
8	An Hermaphrodite	$3^\circ = 8^\square$ Practicus		Lice
9	A beautiful naked man, very strong	$2^\circ = 9^\square$ Theoricus		Frogs
10	A young woman crowned and veiled	$1^\circ = 10^\square$ Zelator / $0^\circ = 0^\square$ Neophyte }		Water turned to Blood

	CXXIII. English of Col. VIII., Lines 1-10	CXXIV. The Heavenly Hexagram.	CXXV.* Seven Hells of the Arabs.	CXXVI. Their Inhabitants.	CXXVII.* Seven Heavens of the Arabs.
1	Dual contending Forces	♃			
2	Hinderers	☿	} Háwiyah	Hypocrites	Dar al-Jalai
3	Concealers	� [♄ Daath]			
4	Breakers in Pieces	♂	Jahim	Pagans or Idolaters	Dar as-Salam
5	Burners	♀	Sakar	Guebres	Jannat al-Maawa
6	Disputers	☉	Sa'ir	Sabians	Jannat al-Khuld
7	Dispersing Ravens	. . . . . .	Hutamah	Jews	Jannat al-Naim
8	Deceivers	. . . . . .	Laza	Christians	Jannat al-Firdaus
9	Obscene Ones	. . . . . .	} Jehannum	Moslems	Jannat al-'adn or al-Karar
10	The Evil Woman or (simply) The Woman	. . . . . .			

TABLE IV (continued)   25

	CXXVIII. Meaning of Col. CXXVII.	CXXIX. Pairs of Angels ruling Wands.	CXXX. Pairs of Angels ruling Cups.	CXXXI. Pairs of Angels ruling Swords.
1	} House of Glory, made of pearls			
2	}	דניאל והואל	איעאל חביוה	ילאל מבהאל
3	}	עממיה חחשיה	ראהאל יבמיה	חריאל הקמיה
4	House of Rest or Peace, made of rubies and jacinths	ניתאל נגאאל	חייאל מומיה	כליאל לאויה
5	Garden of Mansions, made of yellow copper	ילואל וחו	לויה פהליה	אניאל חעמיה
6	Garden of Eternity, made of yellow coral	עלמיה סיטמאל	נלכאל רייאל	רחעאל ייזאל
7	Garden of Delights, made of white diamond	מחשיה ללהאל	מלהאל חהויה	חחהאל מיכאל
8	Garden of Paradise, made of red gold	האאיה נתחיה	וליה ילהיה	ומבאל יחהאל
9	} Garden of Eden, or Everlasting Abode,	שאחיה ירתאל	עריאל כאליה	עניאל מהיאל
10	} made of red pearls or pure musk	אומאל רייאל	מיהאל עשליה	רמביה מנקאל

	CXXXII. Pairs of Angels ruling Coins.	CXXXIII.* Titles and Attributions of the Wand Suit [Clubs]	CXXXIV. Titles and Attributions of the Cup or Chalice Suit [Hearts]
1	. . . . .	The Root of the Powers of Fire	The Root of the Powers of Water
2	ושריה לכבאל	♂ in ♈ The Lord of Dominion	♀ in ♋ The Lord of Love
3	יחויה לחהיה	☉ ♈ Established Strength [Virtue]	☿ ♋ Abundance
4	הוקיה מנדאל	♀ ♈ Perfected Work [Completion]	☽ ♋ Blended Pleasure [Luxury]
5	פויאל מבהיה	♄ ♌ Strife *	♂ ♏ Loss in Pleasure [Disappointment]
6	יילאל נממיה	♃ ♌ Victory	☉ ♏ Pleasure
7	מצראל הרהאל	♂ ♌ Valour	♀ ♏ Illusionary Success [Debauch]
8	כהיאל אבאיה	☿ ♐ Swiftness	♄ ♓ Abandoned Success [Indolence]
9	אלדיה חזיאל	☽ ♐ Great Strength [Strength]	♃ ♓ Material Happiness [Happiness]
10	חהעיה לאויה	♄ ♐ Oppression	♂ ♓ Perfected Success [Satiety]

	CXXXV. Titles and Attributions of the Sword Suit [Spades]	CXXXVI. Titles and Attributions of the Coin, Disc or Pantacle Suit [Diamonds]
1	The Root of the Powers of Air	The Root of the Powers of Earth
2	☽ in ♎ The Lord of Peace Restored [Peace]	♃ in ♑ The Lord of Harmonious Change [Change]
3	♄ ♎ Sorrow	♂ ♑ Material Works [Works]
4	♃ ♎ Rest from Strife [Truce]	☉ ♑ Earthly Power [Power]
5	♀ ♒ Defeat	☿ ♉ Material Trouble [Worry]
6	☿ ♒ Earned Success [Science]	☽ ♉ Material Success [Success]
7	☽ ♒ Unstable Effort [Futility]	♄ ♉ Success Unfulfilled [Failure]
8	♃ ♊ Shortened Force [Interference]	☉ ♍ Prudence
9	♂ ♊ Despair and Cruelty [Cruelty]	♀ ♍ Material Gain [Gain]
10	☉ ♊ Ruin	☿ ♍ Wealth

	CXXXVII. Signs of the Zodiac.	CXXXVIII.* Planets ruling Col. CXXXVII.	CXXXIX. Planets exalted in Col. CXXXVII.	CXXXIXa. Superior Planetary Governers	CXL. Twelve Banners of the Name	CXLI The Twelve Tribes.
15	♈	♂	☉	♀	יהוה	גד Gad
16	♉	♀	☽	☿	יההו	אפראים Ephraim
17	♊	☿	♋	♆	יהחה	מנשה Manesseh
18	♋	☽	♃	♀	חוהי	יששכר Issachar
19	♌	☉	♅	☿	היוח	יהודה Judah
20	♍	☿	☿	♆	הוחי	נפתלי Napthali
22	♎	♀	♄	♀	הויח	אשר Asshur
24	♏	♂	♀	☿	הוחי	דן Dan
25	♐	♃	☋	♆	ויהה	בנימן Benjamin
26	♑	♄	♂	♀	חיהו	זבולן Zebulon
28	♒	♄	♆	☿	הויח	ראובן Reuben
29	♓	♃	♀	♆	חהיו	שמעון Simeon

	CXLII. Angels ruling Houses.	CXLIII. Twelve Lesser Assistant Angels in the Signs	CXXXIX. Angel Lords of the Triplicity in the Signs by Day	CXL. Angel Lords of the Triplicity in the Signs by Night
15	איאל Ayel	שרחיאל Sharhiel	סטרעתן Sateraton	סףעטמאוי Sapatavi
16	טואל Toel	אריזיאל Araziel	ראידאל Rayel	טומת Totath
17	גיאל Giel	סראיאל Sarayel	סערש Sarash	עגנרמען Ogameron
18	כעאל Kael	פכיאל Pakiel	רעדר Raadar	עכאל Akel
19	עואל Oel	שרטיאל Sharatiel	סנחם Sanahem	זלברחית Zalberhith
20	ויאל Veyel	שלתיאל Shelathiel	לסלרא Laslara	סטיא Sasia
22	יחאל Yahel	חדקיאל Chedeqiel	תרגבון Thergebon	אחודראון Achodraon
24	סוסול Susul	סאיציאל Saitziel	בתחון Bethehon	סהקנב Sahaqanab
25	סויעסאל Suyasel	סריטיאל Saritiel	אהוז Ahoz	לברמים Lebarmin
26	כשניעיה Kashenyaiah	שמקיאל Samqiel	סנדלעי Sandali	אלויר Aloyar
28	אנכואל Ansuel	צבמקיאל Tzakmiqiel	עתור Athor	פלאון Polayan
29	פשיאל Pasiel	וכביאל Vakabiel	רמרא Ramara	נתדורינאל Nathdorinel

TABLE V (*continued*) 27

	CXLVI. Angels of the Decantes (Ascendant).	CXLVII. Angels of the Decantes (Succedent).	CXLVIII. Angels of the Decantes (Cadent).
15	זזר Zazer	בההמי Behahemi	סמנרר Satonder
16	כדמרי Kadamidi	מנהראי Minacharai	יכסגנוץ Yakasaganotz
17	סגרש Sagarash	שהדני Shehadani	ביתון Bethon
18	מתראוש Mathravash	רהדיץ Rahadetz	אלינכיר Alinkir
19	לוסנהר Losanahar	זחעי Zachi	סהיבר Sahiber
20	אננאורה Ananaurah	ראידיה Rayadyah	משפר Mishpar
22	טרסני Tarasni	סהרניץ Saharnatz	שהדר Shachdar
24	כמיץ Kamotz	נגדוהר Nundohar	ותרודיאל Uthrodiel
25	משראת Mishrath	והרין Vehrin	אבוהא Aboha
26	מסנון Misnim	יסיסיה Yasyasyah	יסגדיברודיאל Yasgedibarodiel
28	ססßם Saspam	אבדרין Abdaron	גרודיאל Gerodiel
29	בהלמי Bihelami	אורין Avron	סטריף Satrip

	CXLIX. Magical Images of the Decans (Ascendant).	CL. Magical Images of the Decans (Succedent).
15	A tall, dark, restless man, with keen flame-coloured eyes, bearing a sword.	A green-clad woman, with one left bare from the ankle to the knee.
16	A woman with long and beautiful hair, clad in flame-coloured robes	A man of like figure (to the ascendant), with cloven hoofs like an ox.
17	A beautiful woman with her two horses	An eagle-headed man, with a bow and arrow. Wears crowned steel helmet.
18	A man with distorted face and hards, a horse's body, white feet, and a girdle of leaves	A beautiful woman wreathed with myrtle. She holds a lyre and sings of love and gladness.
19	A man in sordid raiment, with him a nobleman on horseback, accompanied by bears and dogs	A man crowned with a white myrtle wreath, holding a bow
20	A virgin clad in linen, with an apple or pomegranate	Tall, fair, large man, with him a woman holding a large black oil jar
22	A dark man, in his right hand a spear and laurel branch and in his left a book	A man, dark, yet delicious of countenance
24	A man with a lance in his right hand, in his left a human head	A man riding a camel, with a scorpion in his hand
25	A man with 3 bodies—1 black, 1 red, 1 white	A man leading cows, and before him an ape and bear
26	A man holding in his right hand a javelin and in his left a lapwing.	A man with an ape running before him
28	A man with bowed head and a bag in his hand.	A man arrayed like a king, looking with pride and conceit on all around him.
29	A man with two bodies, but joining their hand.	A grave man pointing to the sky.

	CLI. Magical Images of the Decans (Cadent).	CLII. Perfumes (Ascendant).	CLIII. Perfumes (Succedent).	CLIV. Perfumes (Cadent).
15	A restless man in scarlet robes, with golden bracelets on his hands and arms	Myrtle	Stammonia	Black Pepper
16	A swarthy man with white lashes, his body elephantine with long legs; with him, a horse, a stag, and a calf	Costum	Codamorns	Cassia
17	A man in mail, armoured with bow, arrows, and quiver	Mastick	Cinnamon	Cypress
18	A swift-footed person, with a viper in his hand, leading dogs	Camphor	Succum	Anise
19	A swarthy hairy man, with a drawn sword and shield	Olibanum	Lyn Balsami	Muces Muscator
20	An old man leaning on a staff and wrapped in a mantle	Santal Flav	Srorus	Mastick
22	A man riding on an ass, preceded by a wolf	Galbanum	Bofor [?]	Mortum
24	A horse and a wolf	Opoponax	As for Asc.	As for Asc.
25	A man leading another by his hair and slaying him	Lign-aloes	Foi Lori	Gaxisphilium
26	A man holding a book which he opens and shuts	Assafœtida	Colophonum	Cubel Pepper
28	A small-headed man dressed like a woman, and with him an old man	Euphorbium	Stammonia	Rhubarb
29	A man of grave and thoughtful face, with a bird in his hand, before him a woman and an ass	Thyme	Coxium	Santal Alb

	CLV. Goetic Demons of Decans by Day (Ascendant).			CLVI. Magical Images of Col. CLV.
15	1	☉	באל Bael	Cat, toad, man, or all at once.
16	4	☋	גמיגין Gamigina	Little horse or ass.
17	7	☋	אמון Amon	(1) Wolf with serpent's tail. (2) Man with dog's teeth and raven's head.
18	10	☿	בואר Buer	Probably a centaur or archer.
19	13	☉	בלאת Beleth	Rider on pale horse, with many musicians. [Flaming and poisonous breath]
20	16	♀	זאפר Zepar	A soldier in red apparel and armour.
22	19	♀	שאלוש Sallos	Solider with ducal crown riding a crocodile.
24	22	♂	יפוש Ipos	Angel with lion's head, goose's feet, horse's tail.
25	25	♂ and ☿	גלאסלבול Glasya-Labolas	A dog with a gryphon's wings.
26	28	♀	ברית Berith	Gold-crowned soldier in red on a red horse. Bad breath.
28	31	☿	פוראש Foras	A strong man in human shape.
29	34	♂	פורפור Furfur	(1) Hart with fiery tail. (2) Angel.

TABLE V (*continued*)   29

			CLVII. Goetic Demons of Decans by Day (Succedent).	CLVIII. Magical Images of Col. CLVII.
15	2	♀	אגאר Agares	Old man, riding a crocodile and carrying a goshawk.
16	5	☿	מארב Marbas	Great Lion.
17	8	♀	ברבמוש Barbatos	Accompanied by 4 noble kings and great troops.
18	11	♀	גוסיון Gusion	"Like a Xenopilus"
19	14	☽	לראיך Leraikha	An archer in green
20	17	♂ and ☿	בוטיש Botis	Viper (or) Human, with teeth and 2 horns, and with a sword.
22	20	☉	פורשון Purson	Lion-faced man riding a bear, carrying a viper. Trumpeter with him.
24	23	♀	אים Aim	Man with 3 heads—a serpent's, a man's (having two stars on his brow), and a calf's. Rides on viper and bears firebrand).
25	26	♀	בים Bimé	Dragon with 3 heads—a dog's, man's, and gryphon's.
26	29	♀	אשתרות Asteroth	Hurtful angel or infernal dragon, like Berith, with a viper [breath bad].
28	32	☉	אסמראי Asmoday	3 heads (bull, man, ram), snake's tail, goose's feet. Rides, with lance and banner, on a dragon.
29	35	☽	מרחיש Marchosias	Wolf with a gryphon's wings and serpent's tail. Breathes flames.

			CLIX. Goetic Demons of Decans by Day (Cadent).	CLX. Magical Images of Col. CLIX.
15	3	♃	ושאגו Vassago	Like Agares.
16	6	♀	ואלפר Valefor	Lion with ass's head, bellowing
17	9	☉	פאימון Paimon	Crowned king on dromedary, accompanied by many musicians.
18	12	♃	שיטרי Sitri	Leapard's head and gryphon's wings.
19	15	♀	אליגוש Eligos	A knight with a lance and banner, with a serpent.
20	18	♀	באתין Bathin	A strong man with a serpent's tail, on a pale horse.
22	21	♂ and ☿	מאראך Marax	Human-faced bull.
24	24	☽	נבר Naberius	A black crane with a sore throat—he flutters.
25	27	♂ and ☽	רינוו Ronove	A monster [probably a dolphin].
26	30	☽	פורנאש Forneus	Sea monster.
28	33	☿	געף Gaap	Like a guide. To be kings.
29	36	♃	ישטולוש Stolas	Raven.

					CLXI. Goetic Demons &c. by Night (Ascendant).	CLXII. Magical Images of Col. CLXI.
15	37	♆		פאניץ	Phenex	Child-voiced phœnix.
16	40	♂		ראום	Raum	Crow.
17	43	♆		שבנוך	Sabnock	Soldier with lion's head rides pale horse.
18	46	♂		ביפרו	Bifrons	Monster.
19	49	♀		כרוכל	Crocell	Angel.
20	52	♀		אלוך	Alloces	Soldier with red leonine face and flaming eyes; rides great horse.
22	55	♃		אוראוב	Orobas	Horse.
24	58	☿		און	Amy	Flaming fire.
25	61	☉ and ☿		זאגן	Zagan	Bull with gryphon's wings.
26	64	♀		האור	Haures	Leopard.
28	67	♀		אמדוך	Amdusias	(1) Unicorn. (2) Dilatory bandmaster.
29	70	♃		שאר	Seere	Beautiful man on winged horse.

					CLXIII. Goetic Demons &c. by Night (Succedent).	CLXIV. Magical Images of Col. CLXIII.
15	38	♂		האלף	Halphas	Stock-dove with sore throat.
16	41	♀		פוכלור	Focalor	Man with gryphon's wings.
17	44	♆		שץ	Shax	Stock-dove with sore throat.
18	47	♀		אואל	Uvall	Dromedary.
19	50	♄		פוך	Furcas	Cruel ancient, with long white hair and beard, rides a pale horse, with sharp weapons.
20	53	☿		כאין	Camio	(1) Thrush. (2) Man with sharp sword seemeth to answer in burning ashes or coals of fire.
22	56	♀		גמור	Gamori	Beautiful woman, with duchess' crown tied to her waist, riding great camel.
24	59	♆		וריאץ	Oriax	Lion on horse, with serpent's tail, carries in right hand two hissing serpents.
25	62	☿		ואל	Volac	Child with angel's wings rides a two-headed dragon
26	65	♆		אנדראלף	Andrealphas	Noisy peacock.
28	68	☉		בליאל	Belial	Two beautiful angels sitting in chariot of fire.
29	71	♀		דנטאל	Dantalion	Man with many countenances, all men's and women's, carries a book in right hand.

TABLE V (*continued*)   31

			CLXV. Goetic Demons &c. by Night (Cadent).	CLXVI. Magical Images of Col. CLXV.
15	39	☿	מאלף Malphas	Crow with sore throat.
16	42	♀	ופאר Vepar	Mermaid.
17	45	♀ and ☉	וינא Viné	Lion on black horse carrying viper.
18	48	☿	חעגנת Haagenti	Bull with gryphon's wings.
19	51	☉	בעלם Balam	3 heads (bull, man, ram), snake's tail, flaming eyes. Rides bear, carries goshawk.
20	54	♀ and ♂	מורם Murmur	Warrior with ducal crown rides gryphon. Trumpeters.
22	57	☿	ושי Oso	Leopard.
24	60	♀	נפול Napula	Lion with gryphon's wings.
25	63	☽	אנדר Andras	Angel with raven's head. Rides black wolf, carries sharp sword.
26	66	☽	כימאור Kimaris	Warrior on black horse.
28	69	☽	דכאוראב Decarabia	A star in a pentacle.
29	72	♂	אנדרומאל Andromalius	Man holding great serpent.

	CLXVII. Egyptian Gods of Zodiac (Asc. Decans).	CLXVIII. Egyptian Names of Asc. Decans	CLXIX. As Col. CLXVII (Succedent)	CLXX. As Col. CXVIII (Succendent).	CLXXI. As Col. CXLVII (Cadent)	CLXXII. As Col. CXLVIII (Cadent)
15	Aroueris	Assicean	Anubis	Lencher	Horus	Asentacer
16	Serapis	Asicath	Helitomenos	Virvaso	Apophis	Aharph
17	Taautus	Thesogar	Cyclops	Verasua	Titan	Tepistosoa
18	Apoltun	Sothis	Hecate	Syth	Mercophta	Thuismis
19	Typhon	Aphruimis	Perseus	Sitlacer	Nephthe	Phuonidie
20	Isis	Thumis	Pi-Osiris	Thoptius	Panotragus	Aphut
22	Zeuda	Serucuth	Omphta	Aterechinis	Ophionius	Arepien
24	Arimanius	Sentacer	Merota	Tepiseuth	Panotragus	Senciner
25	Tolmophta	Eregbuo	Tomras	Sagen	Zeraph	Chenen
26	Soda	Themeso	Riruphta	Epima	Monuphta	Homoth
28	Brondeus	Oroasoer	Vucula	Astiro	Proteus	Tepisatras
29	Rephan	Archatapias	Sourut	Thopibui	Phallophorus	Atembui

	CLXXIII.*
	Genii of the Twelve Hours (Levi).
15	Papus, Sinbuck, Rasphuia, Zahun, Heiglot, Mizkun, Haven
16	Sisera, Torvatus, Nitibus, Hizarbin, Sachluph, Baglis, Laberzerin
17	Hahabi, Phlogabitus, Eirneus, Mascarun, Zarobi, Butatar, Cahor
18	Phalgus, Thagrinus, Eistibus, Pharzuph, Sislau, Schiekron, Aclahayr
19	Zeirna, Tablibik, Tacritau, Suphlatus, Sair, Barcus, Camaysar
20	Tabris, Susabo, Eirnils, Nitika, Haatan, Hatiphas, Zaren
22	Sialul, Sabrus, Librabis, Mizgitari, Causub, Salilus, Jazar
24	Nantur, Toglas, Zalburis, Alphun, Tukiphat, Zizuph, Cuniali
25	Risnuch, Suclagus, Kirtabus, Schachlil, Colopatiron, Zeffar
26	Sezarbil, Azeph, Armilus, Kataris, Razanil, Bucaphi, Mastho
28	Æglun, Zuphlas, Phaldor, Rosabis, Adjuchas, Zophas, Halacho
29	Tarab, Misran, Labus, Kalab, Hahab, Marnes, Sellen

	CLXXIV.
	The Mansions of the Moon.
	[Hindu, *Nakshatra*] Arab, *Manazil*.
15	♈ Sharatan (Ram's head), Butayn (Ram's belly), and 0°-10° Suraya (the Pleiads)
16	♉ 10°-30° Suraya. Dabaran (Alldeboran), and 0°-20° Hak'ah (three stars in head of Orion)
17	♊ 20°-30° Hak'ah, Han'ah (stars in Orion's shoulder), and Zira'a (two stars above ♊)
18	♋ Nasrah (Lion's nose), Tarf (Lion's eye) and 0°-10° Jabhah (Lion's forehead)
19	♌ 10°-30° Jabhah, Zubrah (Lion's mane), and 0°-20° Sarfah (Cor Leonis)
20	♍ 20°-30° Sarfah, 'Awwa (the Dog, two stars in f), and Simak (Spica Virginis)
22	♎ Gafar (φ, ι, and κ in foot of ♍), Zubáni (horns of ♏), and 0°-10° Iklil (the Crown)
24	♏ 10°-30° Iklil, Kalb (Cor Scorpionis), and 0°-20° Shaulah (tail of ♏)
25	♐ 20°-30° Shaulah, Na'aim (stars in Pegasus), and Baldah (no constellation)
26	♑ Sa'ad al-Zábih (the Slaughterer's Luck), Sa'ad al-Bal'a (Glutton's Luck), and 0°-10° Sa'ad al Sa'ad (Luck of Lucks, stars in ♒)
28	♒ 10°-30° Sa'ad al-Sa'ad, Sa;ad al-Akhbiyah (Luck of Tents), and 0°-20° Fargh the former (spout of the Urn)
29	♓ 20°-30° Fargh the former, Fargh the latter (hind lip of Urn), and Risháa (navel of Fish's belly)

TABLE VI   33

	CLXXV. Hebrew Letters.	CLXXVI. Numerical Value of Col. CLXXV.	CLXXVII.* Yetziratic Attribution of Col. CLXXV.	CLXXVII.* Geomantic Intelligences.	CLXXIX. Numbers printed on Tarot Trumps
11	א	1	△	. . . .	0
12	ב	2	☿	רפאל Raphael	1
13	ג	3	☽	גבריאל Gabriel	2
14	ד	4	♀	אנאל Anael	3
15	ה	5	♈	מלכידאל Melchiadel	4
16	ו	6	♉	אסמודאל Asmodel	5
17	ז	7	♊	אמבריאל Ambriel	6
18	ח	8	♋	מוריאל Muriel	7
19	ט	9	♌	ורכיאל Verachiel	11
20	י	10	♍	חמליאל Hamaliel	9
21	כ ך	20 500	♃	סחיאל Sachiel	10
22	ל	30	♎	זוריאל Zuriel	8
23	מ ם	40 600	▽	. . . .	12
24	נ ן	50 700	♏	ברכיאל Barachiel	13
25	ס	60	♐	אדוכיאל Advachiel	14
26	ע	70	♑	הנאל Hanael	15
27	פ ף	80 800	♂	זמאל Zamael	16
28	צ ץ	90 900	≈	כאמבריאל Cambriel	17
29	ק	100	♓	אמניציאל Amnitziel	18
30	ר	200	☉	מיכאל Michael	19
31	ש	300	△	. . . .	20
32	ת	400	♄	כשיאל Cassiel	21
32 bis	ת	400	▽	. . . .	. . . . . .
31 bis	ש	300	⊛	. . . .	. . . . . .

	CLXXX. Title of Tarot Trumps.	CLXXXI. Correct Design of Tarot Trumps.
11	The Spirit of Αιθηρ.	A bearded Ancient seen in profile *
12	The Magus of Power.	A fair youth with winged helment and heels, equipped as a Magician, displays his art *
13	The Priestess of the Silver Star.	A crowned priestess sits before the veil of Isis between the Pillars of Seth *
14	The Daughter of the Mighty Ones.	Crowned with stars, a winged goddess stands upon the moon *
15	The Son of the Morning, chief among the Mighty.	A flame-clad god bearing equivalent symbols *
16	The Magus of the Eternal.	Between the Pillars sits an Ancient *
17	The Children of the Voice: the Oracle of the Mighty Gods.	A prophet, young, and in the Sign of Osiris Risen *
18	The Child of the Powers of the Waters: the Lord of the Triumph of Light.	A young and holy king under the starry canopy *
19	The Daughter of the Flaming Sword.	A smiling woman holds the open jaws of a fierce and powerful lion
20	The Prophet of the Eternal, the Magus of the Voice of Power..	Wrapped in a cloke and cowl, an Ancient walketh, bearing a lamp and staff *
21	The Lord of the Forces of Life.	A wheel of six shafts, whereon revolve the Triad of Hermanubis, Sphinx, and Typhon *
22	The Daughter of the Lords of Truth. The Ruler of the Balance.	A conventional figure of Justice with scales and balances
23	The Spirit of the Mighty Waters.	The figure of an hanged or crucified man *
24	The Child of the Great Transformers. The Lord of the Gate of Death.	A skeleton with a scythe mowing men. The scythe handle is a Tau.
25	The Daughter of the Reconcilers, the Bringer-Forth of Life.	The figure of Diana huntress *
26	The Lord of the Gates of Matter. The Child of the Forces of Time.	The figure of Pan or Priapus *
27	The Lord of the Hosts of the Mighty.	A tower struck by forked lightning *
28	The Daughter of the Firmament. The Dweller between the Waters.	The figure of a water-nymph disporting herself *
29	The Ruler of Flux and Reflux. The Child of the Sons of the Mighty.	The waning moon *
30	The Lord of the Fire of the World.	The Sun *
31	The Spirit of the Primal Fire.	Israfel blowing the Last Trumpet. The dead arising from their tombs *
32	The Great One of the Night of Time.	Should contain a demonstration of the Quadrature of the Circle *
32 bis	. . . .	. . . .
31 bis	. . . .	. . . .

TABLE VI (*continued*) 35

	CLXXXII. The Human Body.	CLXXXIII. Legendary Orders of Being.
11	Respiratory Organs	Sylphs
12	Cerebral and Nervous Systems	"Voices," Witches and Wizards
13	Lymphatic Systems	Lemures, Ghosts
14	Genital System	Succubi
15	Head and Face	Mania, Erinyes [Euminides]
16	Shoulders and Arms	Gorgons, Minotaurs
17	Lungs	Ominous Appearances, Banshees
18	Stomach	Vampires
19	Heart	Horror, Dragons
20	The Back	Mermaids (and ♓, its Zodiacal Opposite), Banshees
21	Digestive System	Incubi, Nightmares
22	Liver	Fairies, Harpies
23	Organs of Nutrition	Nymphs and Undines, Nereids, &c.
24	Intestines	Lamiæ, Stryges, Witches
25	Hips and Thighs	Centaurs
26	Genital System	Satyrs and Fauns, Panic-demons
27	Muscular System	Furies, Chimæras, Boars (as in Calydon), &c.
28	Kidneys, Bladder, &c.	Water Nymphs, Sirens, Lorelei, Mermaids (*cf.* ♍)
29	Legs and Feet	Phantoms, Were-wolves
30	Circulatory System	Will o' the Wisp
31	Organs of Circulation	Salamanders
32	Excretory System	Ghuls, Larvæ, Corpse Candles
32 bis	Excretory Organs, Skeleton	The Dweller of the Threshold, Gnomes
31 bis	Organs of Intelligence	[Socratic Genius]

Editorial Note: The Atus of Thoth

Liber AL, cap. I, v. 57 includes the statement: "All these old letters of my Book are aright: but ץ is not the Star. This also is secret: my prophet shall reveal it to the wise." In Crowley's 'New Comment' on this verse, he observes:

I see no harm in revealing the mystery of Tzaddi to 'the wise'; others will hardly understand my explanations. Tzaddi is the letter of The Emperor, the Trump IV, and Hé is the Star, the Trump XVII. Aquarius and Aries are therefore counter-changed, revolving on the pivot of Pisces, just as, in the Trumps VIII and XI, Leo and Libra do about Virgo. This last revelation makes our Tarot attributions sublimely, perfectly, flawlessly symmetrical. The fact of its so doing is a most convincing proof of the superhuman Wisdom of the author of this Book to those who have laboured for years, in vain, to elucidate the problems of the Tarot.

This substituted attribution is alluded to in various places in *Liber Aleph* and *Magick in Theory and Practice*, but was not spelt out in full in published writings until *The Book of Thoth*. The tables from *777* are based on the old Golden Dawn attributions; to work with the reversed attributions, lines 15 and 28 should be exchanged on all columns based on the Zodiac or Tarot (*i.e.*, VI-VIII, XI, XIV-XX, XXII-XLVII, XLIX, CXXXVII-CLXXIV, CLXXVII-CLXXXIII and CLXXXVI), not all columns throughout as the editors of *777 Revised* state – T.S.

VARIOUS ARRANGEMENTS*

The Naples Arrangement

000	Ain	=	Zero Absolute.
00	Ain Soph	=	Zero as undefinable.
0	Ain Soph Aur	=	Zero as basis of possible vibration.

1	Kether	=	The Point: positive yet indefinable.
2	Chokmah	=	The Point: distinguishable from 1 other.
3	Binah	=	The Point: defined by relation to 2 others.

	The Abyss	=	between Ideal and Actual.

4	Chesed	=	The Point: defined by 3 co-ordinates. Matter.
5	Geburah	=	Motion
6	Tiphareth	=	The Point: now self-conscious, able to define itself in terms of above.
7	Netzach	=	The Point's Idea of Bliss (Ananda).
8	Hod	=	The Point's Idea of Knoweldge (Chit).
9	Yesod	=	The Point's Idea of Being (Sat).

10	Malkuth	=	The Point's Idea of Itself fulfilled in its complement, as determined by 7, 8 and 9.

Suggestive Correspondences from the Hebrew Alphabet†

Aleph   The Holy Ghost—Fool—Knight-Errant. Folly's Doom is Ruin.

Beth   The Messenger. Prometheus. The Juggler with the Secret of the Universe.

Gimel   The Virgin. The Holy Guardian Angel is achieved by Self-sacrifice and Equilibrium.

* [Most of these arrangements are from *The Book of Thoth*.]
† [An earlier version of this appears in Liber LVIII in *Equinox* I (5).]

Daleth	The Wife. Alchemical Salt. The Gate of the Equilibrium of the Universe.
Hé	The Mother is the Daughter, the Daughter is the Mother.
Vau	The Sun. Redeemer. The Son is but the Son.
Zain	The Twins reconciled. The answer of the Oracle is always Death.
Cheth	The Chariot containing Life. The Secret of the Universe. Ark. Sangraal.
Teth	The Act of Power. She who rules the Secret Force of the Universe.
Yod	The Virgin Man. Secret Seed of All. Secret of the Gate of Initiation.
Kaph	The All-Father in 3 forms, Fire, Air, and Water. In the whirlings is War.
Lamed	The Woman justified. By Equilibrium and Self-sacrifice is the Gate.
Mem	The Man drowned in the "womb" flood. The Secret is hidden between the waters that are above and the waters that are below.
Nun	The putrefaction in the Athanor. Initiation is guarded on both sides by Death.
Samekh	The Womb perserving Life. Self-control and Self-sacrifice govern the Wheel.
A'ain	The Exalted Phallus. The Secret of generation is Death.
Pé	The Crowned and Conquering Children emerging from the Womb. The Fortress of the Most High.
Tzaddi	The Husband. Alchemical Sulphur. The Star is the Gate of the Sanctuary.
Qoph	The Womb seething is the glamour of physiological upset which the Sun sleeps. Illusionary is the Initiator of Disorder.
Resh	The Twins shining forth and playing. The fighting of Set and Osiris. In the Sun is the Secret of the Spirit.
Shin	The Stélé. Nuit, Hadit, their God and Man twins, as a pantacle. Resurrection is hidden in Death.
Tau	The Slain God. Universe is the Hexagram.

THE VITAL TRIADS*

The Three Gods I A O	0 The Holy Ghost. I. The Messenger. IX. The Secret Seed.
The Three Goddesses	II. The Virgin. III. The Wife. XVII. The Mother.
The Three Demiurges	X. The All Father 3 in 1. IV. The Ruler. V. The Son (Priest).
The Children Horus and Hoor-Pa-Kraat	VI. The Twins Emerging. XIX. The Sun (Playing). XVI. The Crowned and Conquering Child emerging from Womb in A L P.
The Yoni *Gaudens* (The Woman justified)	VII. The Graal; Chariot of Life. XIV. The Pregnant Womb preserving life. VIII. The Sexually joined.
The Slain Gods	XI. 156 & 666. XII. The Redeemer in the waters. XIII. The Redeeming Belly which kills XV.
The Lingam. The Yoni. The Stèlè (Priest, Priestess, Ceremony)	XV. Erect & Glad. XVIII. The Witch: Yoni stagnant and waiting. XX. God and Man as twins from Nuit and Hadit.
The Pantacle of the Whole	XXI. The System.

---

* [The Roman numbers refer to the numbers printed on the Tarot Trumps in *The Book of Thoth*.]

THE TRIPLICITIES OF THE ZODIAC

Fire
- Fire of Fire. ♈ Lightning—swift violence of onset.
- Air of Fire. ♌ Sun—steady force of energy.
- Water of Fire. ♐ Rainbow—fading spiritualized reflection of the Image.

Water
- Fire of Water. ♋ Rain, Springs, etc.—swift passionate attack.
- Air of Water. ♏ Sea—steady force of putrefaction.
- Water of Water. ♓ Pool—stagnant spiritualized reflection of Images.

Air
- Fire of Air. ♎ Wind—swift onset (note idea of balance as in trade winds).
- Air of Air. ♒ Clouds—steady conveyors of water.
- Water of Air. ♊ Vibrations—bulk unmoved, spiritualized to reflect Ruach (mind).

Earth
- Fire of Earth. ♑ Mountains—violent pressure (due to gravitation).
- Air of Earth. ♉ Plains—steady bearing of life.
- Water of Earth. ♍ Fields—quiet, spiritualized to bear vegetable and animal life.

In each case the Cardinal sign represents the Birth of the Element, the Kerubic sign its Life, and the Mutable sign its passing over towards the ideal form proper to it, *i.e.* to Spirit. So also the Princesses in the Taro are the Thrones of Spirit.

THE TRIPLE TRINITY OF THE PLANETS*

♇	The Spiritual		
☉	The Human (Intellectual)†	} Self (ego)	☿
☽	The Sensory (Bodily)		
♅	The Spiritual		
♄	The Human (Intellectual)†	} Will of the Self	♃
♂	The Sensory (Bodily)		
♃	The Spiritual		
☿	The Human (Intellectual)†	} Relation with the non-ego.	♁
♀	The Sensory (Bodily)		

Middle Pillar

♇	The Spiritual	
☉	The Human	} Consciousness
☽	The Automatic	

Pillar of Mercy

♅	The Creative	
♃	The Paternal	} Mode of action on the non-ego
♀	The Passionate	

Pillar of Severity

♄	The Intuitive	
♂	The Volitional	} Mode of Self-expression.
☿	The Intellectual	

* [This arrangement implies that Neptune has been referred to Kether and Uranus to Chokmah. In the desciption of Atu XXI in *The Book of Thoth*, Crowley attributes Pluto to Kether, Neptune to Chokmah and Uranus to Daäth (see in this connection Crowley's remarks on col. VI, s.v. "Masloth."). It is likely that this arrangement was worked out prior to the discover of Pluto. — T.S.]
† For "intellectual" one might say "conscious".

THE GENETHLIAC VALUES OF THE PLANETS

Neptune	The True Self (*Zeitgeist*). Spiritual environment.
Herschel	The True Will. Spiritual Energy.
Saturn	The Ego (*ahamkara*). Skeleton.
Jupiter	The Higher Love. Wesenschaund of Krause.
Mars	The Bodily Will. Muscular system.
Sun	The Human Will. Vital Force. Spiritual Conscious Self.
Venus	The Lower Love.
Mercury	The Mind. Cerebral tissues and nerves.
Moon	The Senses. Bodily consciousness.

THE ESSENTIAL DIGNITIES OF THE PLANETS*

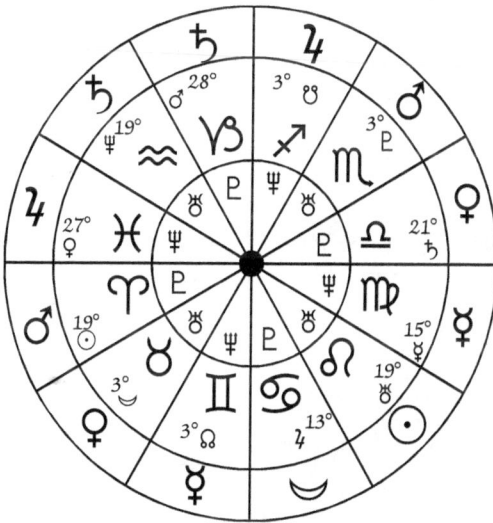

* [This figure is taken from *The Book of Thoth* and represents in diagrammatic form the planetary rulerships (outer ring), exalaltions (middle ring) and "Superior Planetary Governers" (inner ring) of the Zodiac. Cf. Cols. CXXXVII-CXXXIXa.]

NOTES TO TABLE OF CORRESPONDENCES

COL. II: **0-10** are the names of the Numbers or Emanations; **11-32** the Letters spelt in full.

LINE 1.—Some of the common titles of Kether are:—

נקדה פשוח	The Small Point.
תת זל	The Profuse Giver.
נקדה ראשונה	The Primordial Point.
רישא חוורה	The White Head.
אמן	Amen.
אור מופלא	The Hidden Light.
פלא	The Hidden Wonder.
רום מעלה	Inscrutable Height.
אריך אנפין	Long of Nose.
אריך אפים	Long of Face.
יומין	The Ancient of Days.

[Also name of seven inferiors!]

אחיה אשר אחיה	Existence of Existences.
עתיקא דעתיקין	Ancient of Ancient Ones.
עתיקא קדישא	Holy Ancient One.
אור פשוט	The Simple Light.
טמירה דטמרין	Concealed of the Concealed
רישא	*The* Head
אור פנימי	The Inner Light
עליון	The Most High
הוא	He.
רישא דלא	The Head which is Not.

LINE 2.—Chokmah has additional titles:—

כחמה	Power of Yetzirah.[1]
י	of Tetragrammaton.
אבא אב	

It has also the Divine Name, יהוה.

LINE 3.—Binah has these additional titles:—

אמא	The dark sterile mother.
אימא	The bright pregnant mother.
אלהים	
יהוה אלהים	} Divine Names.
כורסיא	Throne.

LINE 4.—Chesed has this additional title:—

כחמה	Majesty.

LINE 5.—Geburah has these additional titles:—

דין	Justice.
פחד	Fear.

LINE 6.—Tiphereth has these additional titles:—

זעיר אנפין	Lesser Countenance.
מלך	King.
שעיר אנפין	*Seir Anpin.*
אדם	Adam.
בן	The Son.
איש	The Man.
שכאנום	Spare Angels.

LINE 9.—Jesod has this additional title:—

צדיק־יסוד־עולם	The Righteous is the Foundation of the World.

LINE 10.—Malkuth has these titles (among others):—

שער	The Gate (by Temurah, עשר = 10).[2]
תרעא	The Gate (Chaldee).

which has the same number (671) as אדני in full—

אלף דלת נון יוד

Also—

Gates of Death.
    "   " Shadow of Death.
    "   " Tears.
    "   " Justice.
    "   " Prayer.
Gate of Daughter of Mighty Ones.
    "   " Garden of Eden.

Also—

Inferior Mother—

The Daughter.	
The Queen.	מלכה
The Bride.	כלה
The Virgin.	בתולה

COL IV.—This column may be equally well symbolized by any single entry, preferably in 0. The Monistic and Nihilistic conceptions are convertible. Hua may be equally named Tao, IAO, Noumenon, and the like. All language on this subject is necessarily feeble and hieroglyphic. It is to name that which by definition has no name.

COL. V.—These God-names are the "Grand Words" of the corresponding grades (see Col. CXXI.) except for 5°=6°, whose G.W. is יחשוה.

42

The Zodiacal Gods are as for the Sephira, which corresponds to the Planet ruling. Apparently, in the numeration of Azbogah, line 12, only the AZ count.

That these following are only titles of the One Ineffable Name is shown by Koran xvii. 110. But monotheism is not true for the normal consciousness, but only for that of the adept.

[99 names of God in Arabic; omitted owing to transcriber's ignorance of that language.]

COL. VI., LINE 31bis.—Essence, *cf. a* and *ω*.

COL. VIII.—

LINES 1-10.—Beth Elohim gives a quite different ten Qliphoth.

LINE 15.—

In the midst of the Zodiacal Qliphoth are סמאל [Samael] and אשמדאי [Asmodai]. At SE corner, Man, Serpent, and the elder Lilith the wife of Samael. At NE corner, the Ox and Ass, and Aggereth the daughter of Machalath. At NW corner, the Scorpion, and אסימון,[3] the Unnameable and עמר נ.[4] At SW angle, the Lion and Horse, and the younger Lilith the wife of Asmodai.

COL. IX.—The Cup of the Stolistes has its rim and 2 and 3 and its foot in 10. The Caduceus is (easily) placed on the Tree and divided into ח, מ, and ש. The Waxing Moon in 4; Waning in 5; Full in 6.

COL. XI.—The elements, of whose nature the signs of the Zodiac partake, are shown by the symbol against them.

COL. XII.—Let 45 be a straight line. On 45 erect the equilateral △s 451, 459. From 4 and 5 draw straight lines 247, 358 ⊥ 45, and the straight lines 25 ⊥ 14, 43 ⊥ 15, 48 ⊥ 59, and 57 ⊥ 49, the points 2, 3, 7 and 8 marking the intersections. Join 19, 12, 13, 23, 78, 79, 89. Let 6 be the point of intersection of 19, 57, 48. On 78 erect an equilateral △ with its apex away from 1. Produce 19 to 10, join 7-10, 8-10. Daath is at the junction of 25, 34. See figure.

COLS. XV.-XVIII.—
Daath—Lavender, Grey-white, Pure violet, Grey flecked gold.
Herschel—Silver flecked white.

COL. XVI, Line 10.—For △, ▽, △, and ▽.

COL. XIX.—Urim and Thummim = Auramoth and Thoum Mou, Egyptian Gods. They are methods of divination by △ and ▽.

COL. XX., LINE 32.—These Gods preside over the pieces in "Rosicrucian Chess."[5]

△ of △	Bishop	Θωοϙͷ ͷωοϙ	
▽ of △	Queen	Ιϵ·ρ̅λοϙρϵθ	
△ of △	Knight	ϵͷωοϙ φωнω	
▽ of △	Pawn	Κλβϵznϵͷϙ	
▽ of △	Castle	ωλϙωϥιϵ·	
✸ of △	King	Φλοͷρω	
△ of ▽	Bishop	ϫοͷιϵ· θλ ͷωοϙ	
▽ of ▽	Queen	Θͷωοͷρ ιϵ· ͷωοͽ	
△ of ▽	Knight	Cϵβλ ͽͷωοϙ ρλοͷρ ιϵ· θλ ͷωοϙ	
▽ of ▽	Pawn	͸ωͷλθθ	
▽ of ▽	Castle	Шнωϵͷ θλ ιϵ·	
✸ of ▽	King	Пθλ ͽλθͷн–ͽнz	
△ of △	Bishop	ϫω ωλͷ	
▽ of △	Queen	ϧͷωοϙ θλ Пϵͽͷͷ	
△ of △	Knight	6·οͷ βλλ	
▽ of △	Pawn	ϫρϵφι	
▽ of △	Castle	Θλρφϵͽϵ· ϥλ ͽͷωοͷθλ пϵ	
✸ of △	King	6·οͽλοͷριϵ·	
△ of ▽	Bishop	ϫρнͷͷϵριϵ·	
▽ of ▽	Queen	Ηιϲϵϵ·	
△ of ▽	Knight	ϵͷωρ	
▽ of ▽	Pawn	ϫϻϵͽϵͷ	
▽ of ▽	Castle	Νϵͷφοͷϻιϵϵ·	
✸ of ▽	King	Ηͽͷωριϵ·	

The Pawns refer to ה as the House of the Elements only, not to ה as ▽.

LINE 32.—Cϥβλͽͷωοϙ ϵͷοͷϵ. Ιϵ·ͷοϻͷωοϙ and ϫρϵφι : ͷͷϻλͷφ: ϫϻϵϲϵͷ : Κλβϵznͷϙ[6]

COL. XXI.—The perfected Egyptian exlaims, "There is no part of me that is not of the Gods." This column gives the attribution in detail. The non-cherubic Zodiac signs are omitted, but follow their affinities.

COL. XXIII.—

Formless State (F)	=	4
Sublime State (S)	=	4
Reflection (R)	=	10
Kashina (K)	=	10
Impurity (I)	=	10
Analysis (A)	=	1
Perception (P)	=	1
		40

COLS. XXXVIII.-XL.—The vagueness and extent of these attributions is shown in this table from Agrippa,[7] who is too catholic to be quite trustworthy.

Things under the Sun which are called Solary

Among stones—

1. The Eye of the Sun.	9. Topazius.
2. Carbuncle.	10. Chrysopassus.
3. Chrysolite.	11. Rubine.
4. Iris (stone).	12. Balagius.
5. Heliotrope (stone).	13. Auripigmentum and
6. Hyacinth (stone).	things of a golden
7. Pyrophylus (stone).	colour.
8. Pantaura.	

Among plants—

1. Marigold.	17. Mastic.
2. Lote-tree.	18. Zedoary.
3. Peony.	19. Saffron.
4. Sallendine.	20. Balsam.
5. Balm.	21. Amber.
6. Ginger.	22. Musk.
7. Gentian.	23. Yellow honey.
8. Dittany.	24. Lignum aloes.
9. Vervain.	25. Cloves.
10. Bay-tree.	26. Cinnamon.
11. Cedar.	27. Calamus.
12. Palm-tree.	28. Aromaticus.
13. Ash.	29. Pepper.
14. Ivy.	30. Frankincense.
15. Vine.	31. Sweet marjoram.
16. Mint.	32. Libanotis.

Among animals—

1. Lion.	5. Boar.
2. Crocodile.	6. Bull.
3. Spotted-wolf.	7. Baboon.
4. Ram.	

Among birds—

1. Phœnix.	5. Cock.
2. Eagle.	6. Crow.
3. Vulture.	7. Hawk.
4. Swan.	

Among insects—

1. Glow-worm.	2. Beetle.

Among fish—

1. Sea-calf.	4. Star-fish.
2. Shell-fish.	5. Strombi.
3. Pullus.	6. Margar.

Among metals—
1. Gold.

COL. XL.—Aaron's breastplate is very doubtful; we advise reliance on columns Stones and Tribes, we having chosen Stones on bases of physical analogy to Signs, Colours, &c.

COL. XLII.—The following table of sub-elemental perfumes is important:—

⊛ of ⊛		Ambergris.
△ of ⊛		The Gall of the Rukh.
▽ of ⊛		Oncha.
▿ of ⊛		Musk.
△ of ⊛		Civet.
⊛ of △		Lign-aloes.
△ of △		Galbanum.
▽ of △		Mastick.
▿ of △		Storax.
△ of △		Olibanum.
⊛ of ▽		Myrrh.
△ of ▽		Camphor.
▽ of ▽		Siamese Benzoin.
▿ of ▽		Indigo.
△ of ▽		Oppoponax.
⊛ of ▿		Dittany of Crete.
△ of ▿		Assafœtida.
▽ of ▿		Clover.
▿ of ▿		Storax.
△ of ▿		Benzoin.
⊛ of △		Saffron.
△ of △		Lign-aloes.
▽ of △		Red-sanders.
▿ of △		Red Sandalwood.
△ of △		Olibanum.

COL. XLIII. and XLIV.—And, generally, all drugs exciting the parts of the body corresponding. See Col. CLXXXII.

COL. XLVI.—Each Trigram combines with itself and the others to make 64 Hexagrams, which partake of the combined nature. This attribution is the true key to the Yi King. No sinologist has had any idea of it, but it is obvious enough now that O.M. has solved it.

See Appendix I.

COL. XLVII.—
LINE 7.—Has a monkey.
LINE **19**.—Said to have a monkey.

COL. XLIX.—The Geomantic Figures of the Planets are those of the signs which they rule.

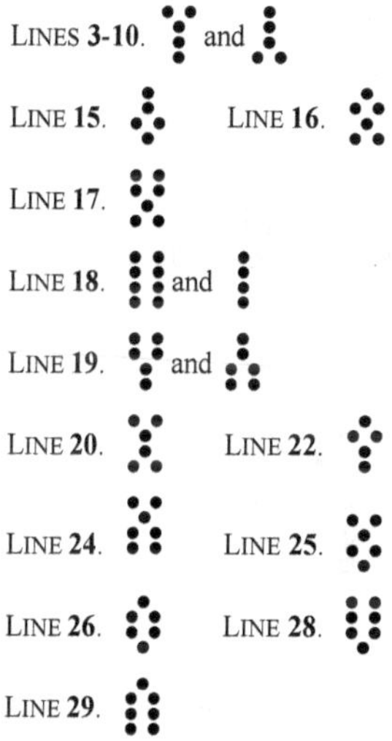
LINES **3-10**. and
LINE **15**.
LINE **16**.
LINE **17**.
LINE **18**. and
LINE **19**. and
LINE **20**.
LINE **22**.
LINE **24**.
LINE **25**.
LINE **26**.
LINE **28**.
LINE **29**.

See the "Handbook of Geomancy," *The Equinox* I: 2, p. 137.[8]

COL. L.—The Catholic "seven deadly sins" in square brackets.

COL. LVII.—Egyptian Quarters.

COLS. LVII., LIX., &c.—Beth Elohim gives:--
Michael, Leo, and South to 🜄 and י.
Gabrial, Bull, and North to 🜂 and ה.
Raphael, Man, and West to 🜃 and ה.
Uriel, Eagle, and East to 🜁 and ו.

COL. LXIX.—

Sattvas,	☿	In a close analogy
Rajas, and	🜍	
Tamas	🜔	

COL. LXXIX., LINE **13**.—
Add (3321) שדברשהמעת שרתתן [Shadbarsheh-moth Sharthathan], the Spirt of the Spirits of the Moon. The final ן is counted as 700, as are the final ם's in Col. LXXVIII., line **13**.[9]

COL. LXXXV.—
LINE **6**.—Or חשמאל.
LINE **9**.—Or זפניאל.

COL. LXXXIX.—Add Daath, חיתא.

COL. XCIII., LINE **10**.—Contains the Earth.

COL. XCVI.—Add Daath, חיוה.

COL. XCIX.—Add among Archangels:—
Azrael, Angel of Death (נ),
Israfel, of Last Trump (ש).

COL. C.—Our order of Angelic Choirs is from R. Mosheh ben Maimon. R. Ishmael and the book Pliah prefer:—

1. Cherubim.
2. Chasmalim.
3. Chaioth.
4. Aralim.
5. Seraphim.
6. Tarshishim.
7. Auphanim. }
8. Auphanim. }
9. Aishim.
10. Taphsarim.

And there are many other schemes.

COL. CII.—Add Daath, אנרי.

COL. CIII.—Add Daath, Cerebrum medium, cuius locus est in parte capitis postica.

But these have many other attributions, and each is itself divisible: thus Chesed and Geburah of Tiphareth are the breasts; Tiphareth the heart; Netzach and Hod the testicles; Jesod the membrum virile; and Malkuth, the anus. The signs of the Zodiac are variously given, and the Planets agree with the face: thus ♄ and ♃, the ears; ♂ and ♀, the nostrils; ☉ and ☽, the eyes; and ☿, the mouth. The hand: thumb, ❂; 1st finger, 🜁; 2nd, 🜄; 3rd, 🜃; 4th 🜂. These, however, vary somewhat.[10]

COL. CVI.—These Abodes are enclosed in four circles: the Waters of Weeping, or Creation, of Oceanus, and the False Sea. Compare the classical four rivers of Hell.[11]

COL. CVIII.—Incomplete and redundant owing to unconentrated nature of Qliphoth.

LINE 2.—Three Evil Forms before Samael are:

קמתיאל [Qemetial]

לביאל [Belial]

עתיאל [Othiel]

The Thaumiel, also called Kerethiel

COL. CIX.—King בלע son of בעור, Dukes עלוה, חמנע, and יתת, are all referred to Daath.

Edomite Kings and Dukes are taken e libro Maggid. and Gen. 36.

COL. CXIV., LINE 1.—*I.e.*, simple breathing without articulation.

COL. CXV.—The furniture, &c., is attributed as told in the ritual, here duly *h—d, c—d,* and *n—r r—d*.[12]

COL. CXXI.—Add the "waiting" Grades of "Lord of the Paths in the Portal of the Vault of the Adept" between the 1st and 2nd Orders; and "Babe of the Abyss" between the 2nd and 3rd.

COL. CXXV.—Burton gives these upside down. The true attribution is checked by the Fire-Worshippers (Guebres) in **5**. Yet, of course, the Kether Hell may be considered as more awful than the Malkuth.

COL. CXXVII.—These and many other (rather far-fetched and irrelevant) attributions of various things are to be found in Burton's *Arabian Nights*, in the Tale of Abn al-Husn and his Slave-Girl Tawaddud.

COL. CXXXIII.—The symbolic forms and Divination meanings of these cards can be readily constructed from considerations of their natures as here indicated.

LINE 5.—This is the First Decan, and begins from Cor Leonis.

COL. CXXXVIII.—Astrological symbols are derived from the primary forms—Cross, Crescent, Circle.

COL. CLXXIII.—For meaning and special function, see original.[13] They should, but do not, accurately refer to the divisions of each sign into 7 planetary parts.

Pietro di Abano[14] gives:—

THE NAMES OF THE HOURS AND THE ANGELS RULING THEM.

The Names of the Hours.

Hours of the day.	Hours of the night.
1. Yayn	Beron
2. Ianor	Barol
3. Nasnia	Thari
4. Salla	Athir
5. Sadedali	Mathon
6. Thamur	Rana
7. Ourer	Netos
8. Tamic	Tafrac
9. Neron	Sassur
10. Iayon	Aglo
11. Abai	Calerua
12. Natalon	Salam

TABLES OF THE ANGELS OF THE HOURS ACCORDING TO THE COURSE OF THE DAYS[15]

Day:	☉	☽	♂	☿	♃	♀	♄
Hour	\multicolumn{7}{c}{(Angels of the Hours of the Day)}						
1.	☉	☽	♂	☿	♃	♀	♄
2.	♀	♄	☉	☽	♂	☿	♃
3.	☿	♃	♀	♄	☉	☽	♂
4.	☽	♂	☿	♃	♀	♄	☉
5.	♄	☉	☽	♂	☿	♃	♀
6.	♃	♀	♄	☉	☽	♂	☿
7.	♂	☿	♃	♀	♄	☉	☽
8.	☉	☽	♂	☿	♃	♀	♄
9.	♀	♄	☉	☽	♂	☿	♃
10	☿	♃	♀	♄	☉	☽	♂
11.	☽	♂	☿	♃	♀	♄	☉
12.	♄	☉	☽	♂	☿	♃	♀
	\multicolumn{7}{c}{(Angels of the Hours of the Night)}						
1.	♃	♀	♄	☉	☽	♂	☿
2.	♂	☿	♃	♀	♄	☉	☽
3.	☉	☽	♂	☿	♃	♀	♄
4.	♀	♄	☉	☽	♂	☿	♃
5.	☿	♃	♀	♄	☉	☽	♂
6.	☽	♂	☿	♃	♀	♄	☉
7.	♄	☉	☽	♂	☿	♃	♀
8.	♃	♀	♄	☉	☽	♂	☿
9.	♂	☿	♃	♀	♄	☉	☽
10.	☉	☽	♂	☿	♃	♀	♄
11.	♀	♄	☉	☽	♂	☿	♃
12.	☿	♃	♀	♄	☉	☽	♂

[The Angels of the Planets according to pseudo-Abano are:—

☉ Michael.
☽ Gabriel.
♂ Samael.
☿ Raphael.
♃ Sachiel.
♀ Anael.
♄ Cassiel.]

Note.—The first hour of the day, of every country, and in every season whatsoever, is to be assigned to the sun-rising, when he first appeareth arising in the horizon. And the first hour of the night is to be the thirteenth hour, form the first hour of the day.

THE YEAR[16]

The Spring: Taloi.
The Summer: Casmaran.
The Autumn: Adarael.
The Winter: Farlas.

The Angels of the Spring: Carcasa, Core, Amatiel, Commissoros.
The Head of the Sign of the Spring: Spugliguel.
The Name of the Earth in the Spring: Amadai.
The Names of the Sun and Moon in the Spring: The Sun, Abrayen; The Moon, Agusita.

The Angels of the Summer: Gargatel, Tariel, Gaviel.
The Head of the Sign of the Summer: Tubiel.
The Name of the Earth in the Summer: Festatui.
The Names of the Sun and Moon in the Summer: The Sun, Athemay; The Moon, Armatas.

The Angels of the Autumn: Tarquam, Gualbarel.
The Head of the Sign of the Autumn: Torquaret.
The Name of the Earth in the Autumn: Rabianira.
The Names of the Sun and Moon in the Autumn: The Sun, Abragini; The Moon, Matasignias.

The Angels of the Winter: Amabael, Ctarari.
The Head of the Sign of the Winter: Altarib.
The Name of the Earth in the Winter: Gerenia.
The Names of the Su and Moon in the Winter: The Sun, Commutaf; The Moon, Affarterim.

COL. CLXXVII.—Musulman attribution of Planets:—

ג ♄
ת ♃
פ ♂
כ ☉
כ and ♀
ב
ד ☿
ר ☽

Note that כ and not ב is the 7th of the double letters.

The Jesuit Kircher gives—

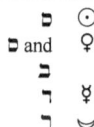

♄	♃	♂	☉	♀	☿	☽
פ	ר	ת	ב	ג	ד	כ

The order of the Planets is that of their apparent rate of motion. By writing them in their order round a heptagon, and tracing the heptagram unicursally, the order of the days of the week is obtained.

COL. CLXXVIII.—These intelligences are angelic in nature, but possessing material and even earthly dominion. Hence they preside over the geomantic figures, whose nature indeed expresses their relation to man.

COL. CLXXXI. —

LINE **11**.—He laughs; bearing a sphere containing illusion in his left hand, but over his right shoulder, and a staff 463 lines long in his right. A lion and a dragon are at his feet, but he seems unaware of their attacks or caresses.

LINE **12**.—His attitude suggests the shape of the Swastika or thunderbolt, the message of God.

LINE **13**.—She is reading intently in an open book.

LINE **14**.—She bears a sceptre and a shield, whereon is figured a dove as a symbol of the male and female forces.

LINE **15**.—His attitude suggests 🜍, and he is seated upon the Cubic Stone, whose sides show the Green Lion and White Eagle.

LINE **16**.—He is crowned, sceptred, and blessing all in a threefold manner. Four living creatures adore him, the whole suggesting a pentagram by its shape.

LINE **17**.—He is inspired by Apollo to prophesy concerning things sacred and progane: represented by a boy with his bow and two women, a priestess and an harlot.

LINE **18**.—He drives furiously a chariot drawn by two sphinxes. As Levi drew it.

LINE 19.—Before him goeth upright the Royal Uræus Serpent.

LINE 21.—[♀, ♃, and ☉, or Sattva, Rajas, and Tamas].

LINE 23.—From a gallows shaped like the letter ┐ hangs by one foot a young fair man. His other leg forms a cross with the suspending one. His arms, clasped behind his head, form an upright △, and this radiates light. His mouth is resolutely closed.

LINE 25.—A winged and crowned goddess, with flashing golden belt, stands, and pours from her right hand the flame of a torch upon an Eagle, while in her left hand she pours water from an horn upon a Lion. Between her feet a moon-shaped cauldron of silver smokes with perfume.

LINE 26.—Levi's Baphomet is sound commentary on this Mystery, but should not be found in the text.

LINE 27.—Human figures thrown thence suggest the letter ע by their attitude.

LINE 28.—A woman, naked, and kneeling on her left knee, pours from a vase in her right hand silver waters into a river, by which grow roses, the haunts of coloured butterfiles. With her left hand she pours golden waters over her head, which are lost in her long hair.

Her attitude suggests the Swastika. Above flashes a great star of seven rays.

LINE 29.—Below, a path leads between two towers, guarded by jackals, from the sea, wherein a Scarabæus marcheth landwards.

LINE 30.—Below is a wall, in front of which, in a fairy ring, two children wantonly and shamelessly embrace.

LINE 31.—An Angel blowing a trumpet, adorned with a golden banner bearing a white cross. Below a fair youth rises from a sacrophagus in the attitude of the god Shu supporting the Firmament. On his left a fair woman, her arms giving the sign of Water—an inverted ▽ on the breast. On his right a dark man giving the sign of Fire—an upright △ on the forehead.

LINE 32.—An ellipse, composed of 400 lesser circles. At the corners of the card a Man, an Eagle, a Bull, and a Lion. Within the circles a naked shining figure in the sign of Earth—right foot advanced, fight hand advanced and raised, left hand lowered and thrown back. The hands grip each a ray of dazzling light, spiril, the right hand being dextro- and the left hand lævo-rotary. A red scarf conceals the fact of male genital organs, and suggests by its shape the letter ך. Such is the conventional hieroglyph.

APPENDIX I

THE TRIGRAMS OF THE YI KING

Attribution to Quarters.	Planetary Attribution.	Hindu Attribution.	Yetziratic Attribution.	Figure.	Name.	Part of body.	Key Scale
S.	☉	Lingam.	+	☰	Khien.	Head.	2 [and 30].
S.E.	♀	Apas.	▽ ם	☱	Tui.	Mouth.	14 [and 23].
E.	♃	Mano (Prana).	☉ ר	☲	Li.	Eyes.	6 [21 and 30].
N.E.	♂	Tejas.	△ ש	☳	Kăn.	Feet.	27 and 31.
S.W.	☿	Vayu.	△ א	☴	Sun.	Thighs.	11 [and 12].
W.	♄	Akasa.	◡ ג	☶	Khân.	Ears.	10 [13 and 32]
N.W.	▽	Prithivi.	▽ ח	☵	Kăn.	Hands.	32 bis.
N.	☽	Yoni.	○ ח	☷	Khwăn.	Belly.	3 and 13.

The Trigrams should be considered as the symbols which combine these meanings, the Hexagrams as combinations of these, chosen according to circumstances. Thus ䷜ is Fire of ☽, or Energy of ♄, and might mean beginning to change, or force applied to obstruction, as it actually does.

49

THE HEXAGRAMS OF THE YI KING.

	Figure.	Nature.	Name.	Divination and Spiritual Meaning.
1		+ of +	*Kh*ien	Heaven, &c. (+ for Lingam.)
2		○ of ○	Khwăn	Earth, &c. (○ for Yoni.)
3		⌣ of △	*K*un	Danger and obscurity—γενος.
4		▽ of ⌣	Măng	Youth and ignorance.
5		⌣ of +	Hsü	Waiting, sincerity.
6		+ of ⌣	Sung	Contention, opposition, strength in peril.
7		○ of ⌣	Sze	Multitude, age and experience.
8		⌣ of ○	Pî	Help.

Figure.	Nature.	Name.	Divination and Spiritual Meaning.
9	△ of +	Hsiâo Khû	Small restraint.
10	+ of ▽	Lî	Pleased, satisfaction, treating, attached to, a shoe.
11	○ of +	Thâi	Spring, tree course.
12	+ of ○	Phî	Decay, patience, obedience, autumn, shutting up, restriction
13	+ of ☉	Thung Zăn	Union (of men).
14	☉ of +	Tâ Yû	Great havings.
15	○ of ▽	Khien	Humility.
16	△ of ○	Yü	Harmony and satisfction.

Figure.	Nature.	Name.	Divination and Spiritual Meaning.
17	▽ of △	Sui	Following
18	▽ of △	Kû	Troublesome services, arrest of decay, hard work.
19	○ of ▽	Lin	Approach of authority, inspect, comfort.
20	△ of ○	Kwân	Manipulating, contemplating.
21	⊙ of △	Shih Ho	Union by gnawing, legal constraint.
22	▽ of ⊙	Pî	Ornament, freewill.
23	▽ of ○	Po	Overthrow, couch.
24	○ of △	Fû	Returning, visit from friends.

Figure.	Nature.	Name.	Divination and Spiritual Meaning.
25	+ of △	Wû Wang	Simplicity and sincerity, earnestness.
26	▽ of +	Tâ *Khû*	Great accumulation.
27	▽ of △	Î	Nourishment, upper jaw.
28	▽ of △	Tâ Kwo	Great carefulness, weak beam.
29	⩗ of ⩗	Khan	Pit, defile, peril.
30	☉ of ☉	Lî	Inherent in, attached to, docility.
31	▽ of ▽	Hsien	Influencing to action, all, jointly.
32	△ of △	Hăng	Perseverance, keeping to the path.

	Figure.	Nature.	Name.	Divination and Spiritual Meaning.
33		+ of ▽	Thun	Returning, avoiding, retirement.
34		△ of +	Tâ Kwang	Violence, the Great Ram.
35		⊙ of ○	Tzin	To advance (good).
36		○ of ⊙	Ming Î	Intelligence, wounded.
37		⊜ of ⊙	Kiâ Zăn	Household, wifely duty.
38		⊙ of ▽	Khwei	Disunion, family discord.
39		⊽ of ▽	Kien	Lameness, immobility, difficulty.
40		△ of ⊽	Kieh	Unravelling (a knot, &c.).

	Figure.	Nature.	Name.	Divination and Spiritual Meaning.
41		▽ of ▽	Sun	Diminution.
42		△ of △	Yî	Addition, increase.
43		▽ of +	Kwâi	Displacing, strength, complacency, tact.
44		+ of △	Kâu	Unexpected event, a bold woman.
45		▽ of ○	Tzhui	Collected, docility.
46		○ of △	Shăng	Advance and ascent.
47		▽ of ☉	Khwăn	Straightened, distressed, ⁚⁚ Carcer, growth restricted.
48		◡ of △	Tzing	A well, self-cultivation.

	Figure.	Nature.	Name.	Divination and Spiritual Meaning.
49		▽ of ☉	Ko	Change
50		☉ of △	Ting	A caldron, a concubine, flexibility, quick ear and eye.
51		△ of △	Kăn	Ease, development, moving power, thunder.
52		▽ of ▽	Kān	Peace, a mountain.
53		△ of ▽	Kien	Fortunate marriage, gradual advance, goose.
54		△ of ▽	Kwei Mei	Unfortunate marriage (of a younger sister before the elder).
55		△ of ☉	Făng	Large, abundant, progress.
56		☉ of ▽	Lü	Strangers.

Figure.	Nature.	Name.	Divination and Spiritual Meaning.
57	△ of △	Sun	Flexibility, penetration, vacillation, wind, wood, &c.
58	▽ of ▽	Tui	Pleasure, help from friends, still water.
59	△ of ◡	Hwân	Dissipation, dispersion, turning to evil.
60	◡ of ▽	Kieh	Joints of body, regular division.
61	▽ of ◡	Kung fù	Inmost sincerity.
62	△ of ▽	Hsiao Kwo	Non-essential, success of trifles, a wonded bird, small divergences.
63	◡ of ☉	Ki Tzi	Help attained, complete success.
64	☉ of ◡	Wei Tzi	Incomplete success, foolish impulse, failure.

EXPLANATIONS OF THE ATTRIBUTIONS
IN THE MORE IMPORTANT COLUMNS OF TABLES I-VI.

COLUMN I: THE KEY SCALE

In order to understand thoroughly the Key Scale, the student should have mastered the Essay on the Qabalah, (*Equinox* I (5), pp. 72-89), and acquainted himself with the use of Liber D (*Equinox*, I (8), Supplement).*

It should be sufficient therefore in this place to explain simply the significance of the symbols of this scale.

The numbers **000** to **10** are printed in heavy block type. They refer to the three forms of Zero and the ten Sephiroth or numbers of the decimal scale. The diagram shows the conventional geometrical arrangement of the symbols 1-10. The numbers 11-32 correspond to the 22 letters of the Hebrew alphabet. They are attributed to the paths which join the Sephiroth. Their arrangement is shown in the same diagram. 31 and 32 must be supplemented by 31-bis and 32-bis, as these two paths possess a definitely double attribution; viz. 31-bis to Spirit as against 31 to Fire; 32-bis to Earth as against 32 to Saturn.

The numbers 11, 23, 31, 32-bis, 31-bis are printed close to the left edge of the column for convenience of reference, they referring to the 5 elements.

12, 13, 14, 21, 27, 30, 32 are printed in the centre of the column: they refer to the planets.

15, 16, 17, 18, 19, 20, 24, 25, 26, 28, 29 are printed on the right-hand edge of the column. They refer to the signs of the Zodiac.

* [Both these texts were reprinted in *The Qabalah of Aleister Crowley* (later *777 and other Qabalistic Writings*), the former under the spurious title "Gematria," the latter in a slightly abridged form. — T.S.]

It should be understood that the main object of this book is to enable the student to do four things. Firstly, to analyze any idea soever in terms of the Tree of Life. Secondly, to trace the connection between every class of idea referring it thereto. Thirdly, to translate any unknown symbolism into terms of any known one by its means. Fourthly, to make a concatenation of any part of any idea with the rest by analogy with the similar concatenation of the Sephiroth and the paths.

In this connection, observe that the numbers (of this column) subsequent to 10 are not to be considered as real numbers. The figures have been assigned to them arbitrarily for convenience only. Thus there is no special sympathy between 11 and the letter Aleph which is referred to it. For Aleph is connected chiefly with the idea of Zero and Unity, whereas 11 is the number of Magick, and its principal alphabetical correspondences are Beth and Teth. Further, the essential definition of a path is determined by its position on the Tree of Life as conductor of the influence of the Sephiroth which it connects.

One great difficulty in constructing this table is caused by the intimate correspondency between certain Sephiroth and paths. Thus Kether is directly reflected into Chokmah according to one mode, and into Tiphareth according to another. Further, the creative energy on a still lower plane is symbolized in Yesod. In respect of its unity, moreover, it has its analogy in the 11th path.

In the case of Chokmah the difficulty is even greater. Chokmah, as the creative energy Chiah, is of the same nature as Chesed, and even Tiphareth as Vau shows an intimate correspondence with the final Hé of Tetragrammaton as Chokmah with her mother. Among the paths of the Serpent this creative energy is expressed according to various modes: by the 11th path, the Wandering Fool, who impregnates the King's Daughter, by the 12th path which creates Maya, the 15th which is definitely phallic,* and even the 13th which symbolizes change through putrefaction. Lastly, he is found in this function in the 27th path, which

---

* [This is a probably a reference to the attribution of Aries and the Tarot Trump the Emperor to the 15th Path, as opposed to the later attribution of Aquarius and the Star. — T.S.]

represents *Phallum Ejaculentem*. Chokmah being pre-eminiently the causer of change.

Again, Chokmah is the Logos, the messenger, the transmitter of the influence of Kether, and this is shown, in a lower mode, in the Sephira Hod. He is also implied in the 11th path, for the Fool also transmits the essence of Kether. He is in the 12th path as the Magician, Mercury, in the 16th as the Magus of the Eternal, in the 17th as the Oracle of the Mighty Gods, and in the 20th as the Prophet of the Eternal, the Magus of the Voice of Power.* The idea of the message is also implied in the 13th and 25th paths, perhaps even in the 32nd. The 18th path, too, conveys a certain quintessence although not in a Mercurial manner. And it is just these subtle distinctions which are vital to the proper understanding of the Tree of Life.

The idea of Binah is even more complicated. Her darkness is referred to Saturn. As the Great Sea, she gives her nature to all those paths which contain the idea of the element of Water. Binah is connected with the Azoth, not only because the Azoth is the lower Moon, but because the Azoth partakes also of the Saturnian character, being the metal lead in one of the Alchemical systems. She is also the Great Mother. She is Venus and she is the Moon, and in each aspect she sheds her influence into very various paths. We need not here go further into the cases of the other Sephiroth.

Now from a practical point of view of consturcting these tables, it will evidently be very difficult in many cases to choose on which path to place any given idea. It is obvious, for instance, that the Lotus— which is also a Wheel—might be attributed to any path in respect ot its femininity. In some cases it has been necessary to give several attributions to the same thing. Observe in particular the 12 different aspects of Isis. The student must not attempt to use this book as if it were Molesworth. The whole idea of these tables is to supply him with very varied information, in such a form that he can build up in himself a scheme of the Universe in an alphabet, at once literary and

---

* [These are Golden Dawn titles of the Tarot Trumps popularly known as the Hierophant, the Lovers and the Hermit respectively. See Col. CLXXX. — T.S.]

mathematical, which will enable him to obtain a coherent conception of the Universe in a sufficiently compact and convenient form to utilize in both his theoretical and practical working.

COLUMNS II, III: THE HEBREW NAMES OF NUMBERS AND LETTERS

These columns indicate the principlal moral ideas connected with the Sephiroth. The names of the letters indicated rather the pictorial glyph suggests by the shape of the letter. But they also conceal a secondary meaning behind that of the numerical value and the number of the Tarot Trump of each. The value of the name of each letter modifies that meaning. For example, Aleph, while principally significant of Zero and Unity, explains itself further by the number 111, the value of the letters A L P. That is to say a study of the number 111 enables us to analyze the meaning of the number 1. It indicates, for instance, the trinitarian equation $1 = 3$.

Note that the letters Hé and Vau may each be spelt fully in four different ways, corresponding to the four worlds given in column LXIV.

It is to be thoroughly understood that the titles of the Sephiroth make no claim to give anything like a complete description of their nature. The glyphs of the 22 letters have some times a greater, some times a less, importance in elaborating the connotation.

ALEPH   means an *Ox*, principally because the shape of the letter suggests the shape of a yoke. There is also a reference to the mildness and patience of Harpocrates: indeed, to his sexual innocence. The function of ploughing is clearly the chief idea involved: herein lies a paradox—to be studied in the last act of *Parsifal*.

BETH   is a *House*, the letter showing the roof, floor, and one wall. It is the dwelling place of man in the world of duality and illusion.

GIMEL   the Camel, reminds us of the position of the Path on the Tree of Life as joining Kether and Tiphereth, and thus the means of travelling through the wilderness of the Abyss.

DALETH   a *Door*, refers to the position of the path as joining Chokmah and Binah. It is the gate of the Supernals. Again, it is the letter of Venus and shows the sexual symbolism. The shape suggests the porch of a doorway, or a porched tent-flap.

HÉ   a *Window*, remindes us that Understanding (Hé being the letter of the Mother in Tetragrammaton) is the means by which the Light reaches us. The gap between the two strokes is the window.

VAU   a *Nail* (shape directly hieroglyphic) suggests the fixation of the Supernals in Tiphereth.

ZAYIN   a *Sword*, refers to the attribution of the letter to Gemini, the sign corresponding to intellectual analysis. The Yod above suggests the hilt; that below, the blade.

CHETH   a *Fence*. The Cross-bar on the uprights suggests a fence— more properly the Holy Graal.

TETH   is a *Serpent*, as is very obvious from the shape of the letter. The symbol of Leo also resembles the Uræus. It being the house of the Sun, the idea is to emphasize the identity of the Star and the Snake.

YOD   a *Hand*, indicates the means of action. The doctrine is that the Universe is set in motion by the action of indivisible points (Hadit). The Hand being the symbol of creative and directive energy, is the polite equivalent of Spermatozoon, the true glyph.

KAPH   the *Palm* of the hand, is the hub of the wheel from whcih the force of the 5 elements spring. The reference is particulalry to Jupiter and the 10th ATU. The regular form may suggest the fist: the final, the open hand.

LAMED   an *Ox-Gods*, is once more principally a matter of shape. There is, in particular, a reference to the relation of Lamed with Aleph, a matter too profound to discuss in this place. It might be studied personally in the light of *The Book of the Law* and of essays thereon.

MEM   *Water* suggests a wave; a breaker by its initial or medial form, and still water by its final form. In this single case, the actual meaning of the word is identical with the Yetziratic attribution of the letter. Note that the letter NUN, meaning fish, is not attributed to Pisces but to Scorpio.

NUN   a *Fish*, is that which lives and moves in the water: which is here a symbol of death. It therefore indicates the forces of Scorpio, generation through putrefaction. The final form suggests a tadpole.

SAMECH   a *Prop*, refers to the fact that the path connects Tiphereth with Yesod and therefore serves to connect Microprosopus with his foundation. The shape may suggest a pillow, or a stone, to be thrust under some object.

A'AIN   an *Eye*, refers to the meatus. This explains the application of Capricornus to the 15th ATU. The shape may suggest the two eyes and the nose.

PÉ   a *Mouth*, is explained by the shape of the letter. The Yod represents the tongue.

TZADDI   a *Fish Hook*, is also an obvious matter of shape.

QOPH   the *Back of the Head*. The shape is fairly suggestive.

RESH   a *Head reversed*. The seat of the human consciousness, which is Solar, pertaining to Tiphereth, is in the head. Resh is the Solar letter. In shape it is merely a big Yod, implying the brain as the expansion of the Spermatozoon.

SHIN   a *Tooth*, plainly exhibits the three fangs of a molar. It is also a glyph of the triple tongue of flame, the letter being referred to the element of Fire. The suggestion of devouring, eating, or eating into, is also given. The idea of the ternary shown by the three Yods is borne out by the value of the letter, 300. Yet the letter being one letter, the doctrine of the Trinity is implied. Hence its secondary attribution to the element of Spirit. It is also a glyph of the God SHU, whose head and arms, separating SEB and NUIT, form the letter. This connects it with the fire of the Last Judgement (ATU XX). I may here note that SHU is the God of air and not of fire, of the firmament that separates Earth and Heaven; so that the idea of the letter is to establish a link between the ideas of fire and air, the two active elements. There is a similar connection between Mem and Tau. The 12th ATU shows a man hanging from a cross, which is the meaning of Tau.

TAU   a *Tau* or *Cross* symbolizes the element of Earth aas a solidification of the four elements. There is also a phallic meaning, whence Tau is attributed not only to Earth, but to Saturn. Tau was originally written cruciform.

I may supplement the above remarks by saying that they make clear that there is no such apodeictic connection between the letters as between the numbers. The meanings are in many cases little more than indications of certain lines on which meditation may be profitably pursued.

COLUMN V: GOD NAMES IN ASSIAH

1. EHEIEH. The God names of the Sephiroth refer, for the most part, by meaning to their characteristics. Thus EHEIEH, pure existence, belongs to 1. The sound of the word represents the indrawn and outdrawn breath.

2. YAH gives the title of the Father.

3. JEHOVAH ELOHIM gives the full name of the God, as if the Supernals were collected in Binah.

4. The name AL is used in many senses. Its deepest sense is give by *The Book of the Law*. The excuse for writing it here is that 4 represents Jupiter, the highest possible manifestion of Deity.

5. ELOHIM GIBOR. The attribution is natural.

6. JEHOVAH ELOAH VA-DAATH. The reference is to Tiphereth as the child of Chokmah and Binah, Daäth (their first child) having failed to find a place on the Tree.

7-8. JEHOVAH TZABAOTH and ELOHIM TZABAOTH give respectively the two principal names of the Demiurge expressed in multiplicity and positive action. (Hosts.)*

* [See in this connection I.Z.Q. 740-745. — T.S.]

9. SHADDAI EL CHAI. Almighty and Ever-living God: refers to his function as Pangenetor.

10. ADONAI MELEKH. "My Lord the King" is the natural inhabitant of "The Kingdom."

The attributions of the Elemental Gods are somewhat arbitrary. Tetragrammaton is given to Air (11), because Jehovah is Jupiter, the Lord of Air. Al is given to Water (23), because of its attribution to Chesed, the Sephira of Water. Elohim is given to Fire (31) because the name of five letters represents the active but feminine principle Shakti of Geburah, the fiery Sephira. Adonai ha-Aretz is the natural title of Earth (32-bis); and Adonai is the name of God particularly referred to man in his mortality. It is one title of the Holy Guardian Angel. Yeheshua is attributed to Spirit (31-bis) on account of the formation of the word from Tetragrammaton by the insertion of the letter Shin, thus forming the Pentagram of the Elements. The planetary names refer to the sacred numbers of the planets. The Zodiacal signs are not honoured with God-names in the Hebrew system. Those referring to the planets ruling them may be used.

COLUMN VI: THE HEAVENS OF ASSIAH

This column gives the names of the astral or apparent phenomena corresponding to Column II. It must be understood that in speaking of the sphere of a planet the astrological attribution is a minor quasi-accidental and not necessarily reliable function. It depends on astrological theories. By "Tzedeq" we should understand any function of a phenomenon which partakes of the nature of Jupiter. At the same time the Heavens of Assiah do not refer directly to pure number but indirectly through the astrological and cosmographical conventions.

1. RASHITH HA-GILGALIM. The primum mobile—or "beginning of whirling motion"—tells us that Kether is the point from which we measure motion. The Sephiroth might even perhaps be considered as co-ordinate axes.

2. MASLOTH. The fixed stars are connected with the idea of Hadit as positive interruptions of the negative continuum Nuit. Neptune is

attributed to this sphere as being the outpost of the Solar System. Uranus is attributed to Daäth because of its explosive nature. The Abyss is represented in Nature by the Asteroids. There is another aspect of Uranus, the Magical Will, which is assigned to Chokmah. There is also another of Neptune, whose astrological characteristics are sympathetic with Neschamah and therefore with Binah. It must be remarked that since above the Abyss a thing is only true so far as it contains its contradictions in itself, the attributions of the planets above the Abyss cannot be so definite as those below. Each of them can in a way be attributed to any of the Supernals, and each may be given to any one for contradictory reasons. It cannot be too strongly pointed out to the practical Magician that when he comes to work with ideas above the Abyss, the whole character of his operations is completely changed.

3. SHABATAI represents Saturn as the planet of repose, of darkness, and perhaps as the category of Time. Note that Saturn is attributed to Daäth in the hexagram of the planets. This is the creative Saturn, the hidden God, and the Daäth of the apex of the upper triangle of the hexagram is in reality a concentration of the Trinity of the Supernals. The hexagram must not be like "the Stooping Dragon," crowned with a falsity.

4. TZEDEQ means righteousness; the inexorable law of Jupiter. The connection of this with the number 4 depends on the aspect of 4 as the square of 2, the limitation of the Dyad further fixed by self-multiplication, the introduction of a new dimension. 4 is thus a number of rigidity or materiality. Hence its ideal quality is inexorable righteousness. Yet in connection with this, remember that Chesed means Mercy and 4 is Daleth, the letter of Venus, Love. Consideration of this is very helpful in understanding the way in which a Sephira combines widely diverse ideas.

5-9. 5. MADIM. 6. SHEMESH. 7. NOGAH. 8. KOKAB. 9. LEVANAH.*

10. CHOLIM YESODOTH. The sphere of the elements is attributed to Malkuth. Of course, the elements extend throughout the Sephiroth. But

---

* Editorial Note.—The explanatory notes on these five heavens of Assiah were never written. The typescript merely has "Look up the actual meaning."

"element" here means the composition of Nephesch and sensible matter; which pertain to Malkuth.

THE ELEMENTS

11. RUACH means air, also breath and mind, thought being the expression in expansion of the union of Chokmah and Binah in the subconscious. Ruach is also translated Spirit—Latin *Spiritus*. There must be no confusion between this "spirit" and that symbolized by the letter Shin. The distinctions are of the utmost importance, and so manifold and subtle that the subject demands a complete essay in itself.

23. MAIM is Hebrew for Water.

31. ASH is the Hebrew for Fire.

32 bis. ARETZ is the Hebrew for Earth.

31 bis. ATH. I have myself* assigned the word Ath to the of Spirit as an element, it being the Alpha and Omega, or the essence which interpenetrates the other elements. It is the unformulated realitry common to them, by virture whereof they exist.

The planetary heavens follow their Sephirotic attributions; *e.g.* 27, the Heaven of Mars is Madim given above against the number 5.

The Zodiacal heavens are simply the Hebrew names of the signs.

COLUMN VII: ENGLISH OF COLUMN VI

The nature of the entries in this column is to be studied in the light of the traditional astrological conception.

COLUMN VIII: ORDERS OF QLIPHOTH

The titles of the Qliphoth, generally speaking, suggest the vice characteristic of the Sephira or other idea to which they are attributed. Thus the Thaumiel refer to Ketherm because their characteristic is to possess two contending heads, and so to deny the unity of Kether. So also the Golachab are giants like volcanoes, symbolizing energy and

---

* [No you didn't Aleister, the G.D. did: see for example the explanation of the "Pyramid of the Elements" admission badge in the Philosophus ritual. — T.S.]

fire, and their liability to appear as tyranny and destruction. Similarly the Qliphoth of Venus are carrion birds, as opposed to the dove, sparrow, etc.

The transliteration and meaning of the Hebrew names of the Orders of Qliphoth are as follows:—

	QEMETIEL.	Crowd of Gods.
0.	BELIA'AL.	Worthlessness.
	A'ATHIEL.	Uncertainty.*
1.	THAUMIEL.	Twins of God.
2.	GHAGHIEL.	Hinderers.
3.	SATARIEL.	Hiding.
4.	GHA'AGSHEKLAH.	Smiters.
5.	GOLACHAB.	Flaming Ones.
6.	THAGIRIRON.	The Litigation.
7.	A'ARAB ZARAQ.	The Ravens of Dispersion.
8.	SAMAEL.	The False Accuser.
9.	GAMALIEL.	The Obscene Ass.
10.	LILITH.	The Woman of Night.
15.	BA'AIRIRON.	The Flock.
16.	ADIMIRON.	Bloody.
17.	TZALALIMIRON.	Clangers.
18.	SHICHIRIRON.	Black.
19.	SHALEHBIRON.	Flaming.
20.	TZAPHIRIRON.	Scratchers.
22.	A'ABIRIRON.	Clayey.
24.	NECHESHTHIRON.	Brazen.
25.	NECHESHIRON.	Snakey.
26.	DAGDAGIRON.	Fishy.
28.	BAHIMIRON.	Bestial.
29.	NASHIMIRON.	Malignant Women.

* [This attribution is highly questionable: it may be doubted whether any meaningful Qliphothic attribution is possible here, outside the Sephirothic system. In *Kabbala Denudata* (tom. I. pars. IV. fig xvi. (Z)), these three names are referred to Kether, Chokmah and Binah respectively. — T.S.]

COLUMN X: MYSTIC NUMBERS OF THE SEPHIROTH

These numbers are obtained byadding together the natural numbers up to and including the one in question. Thus, the sum of the first ten is fifty-five. Their significance has been well worked-out; and is important up to the number 13. After that, the numbers 15, 20, 21, 24, 28 and 31 have repaid the study bestowed upon them.

For the meaning of the primes from 11 to 97 see page 132.

COLUMN XI: THE ELEMENTS, WITH THEIR PLANETARY RULERS

Kether is said to be the root of Air, because as the force of air, or the balance of Fire and Water, and, as connected, it is Aleph, with the ideas of Zero and Unity. Chokmah is said to be the root of Fire, because of its creative nature; Binah of Water, because of its receptive passivity, and its symbolism as the Great Sea.

The three elements are refelcted into the second triad, Water being referred to Chesed, partly because it is the recipient of the male influence of the Supernals, partly because 4 is Daleth, Venus, the feminine or watery principle. The energy and mobility of Geburah naturally suggests Fire. The third member of the triad, Tiphereth, is Air,* partly for the same reason as Kether just cited, partly because Tiphereth is Microprosopus, who is Vau in Tetragrammaton, Vau being the letter of Air, the result of the union of Yod and Hé, Fire and Water.

In the third triad Netzach is Fire, as representing the devouring quality of love: Hod, Water, as representing the reflecting quality of thought: and Yesod, Air, on account of the extremely important mystery expressed in Liber 418, Æthyr XI (see *Equinox* I (5), Supplement). The integrity of the Sephiroth is guaranteed by the fact that each one contains its contradictory in itself. Yesod, the Foundation, the principle of stability, cannot be shaken because it is also the idea of elasticity, and instability.

---

* [The printed edition reads "... of Geburah naturally suggests Fire and Air. The third member of the triad is Tiphereth" which appears to be corrupt; the present reading is a conjectural restoration. — T.S.]

Earth appears for the first time in Malkuth. The three active elements are represented in three triads in a progressively diluted and impure form. There is a progressive admixture of ideas as one descends the Tree; but when the descent becomes so gross that they can no longer subsist as such, they unite to act as a trinity, to reproduce themselves by reflection or crystallisation as a fixed form in which their original natures are no longer perceptible as such. They merely modify the character of the compound. The analogy is to chemical elements, which are unable to manifest the natural property of the pure state in a compound. It is only their subtler qualities which influence the nature of the compound. Thus none of the physical properties of H. are directly to be observed in its combination with SO_4. It is only the subtler qualities which determine that H_2SO_4 should be an acid.

The attribution of Earth to Malkuth is important as explaining the nature of Nephesch and manifested matter. It is to be understood that the three active elements and the first 9 Sephiroth do not exist at all directly for the senses. They are to be apprehended only indirectly, by observing their function through determining the nature of sensible things. The necessary attributions* of this column are extremely important as throwing light on the nature of the Heavens of Assiah. They must be studied and meditated with great care.

Thus the fiery signs Aries, Leo, and Sagittarius partake of the nature of Sol and Jupiter, because of the active, lordly, creative, paternal, generous, noble and similar qualities. The earthy signs are sympathetic with Venus and Luna because of the passive receptivity of those planets. Airy signs correspond particularly with Saturn and Mercury, because of the connection of these planets with thought. Watery signs are sympathetic with Mars with regard to the fact that Water possesses the fiery property of breaking up and destroying solids. The student must be careful to avoid expressing himself by inventing false

---

* [The text at this point, following the printed edition, appears corrupt. Either the word "necessary" is wrong or there is material missing after "necessary"; the adjective before "attributions" should be something along the lines of "Zodiacal" or "remaining." — T.S.]

antinomies. There is a great danger in arguing backwards in the
Qabalah, especially in the case of attributions of this sort. Thus the
explanation of the martial nature of water must not be used to argue a
watery nature in Mars, whose natural sympathy is evidently Fire.

It would be supremely misleading to try to obtain any information
about the nature of Mars from this column. It is almost impossible to
suggest any rule for avoiding errors of this sort. The best I can do is to
recommend the student never to lose sight of the fact that all
attributions whatsoever have no absolute quaility. The object is really
to remind the student of what he already knows about any given idea
and its relation with the rest. He should therefore determine for himself
the nature of any idea principally by meditation or direct magical
investigation, such as actual visions. He may accept provisionally the
validity of correspondences so far as they indicate the best methods of
invocation and evocation. Having thus firmly established in his head
the correspondences of a symbol, he is less likely to misinterpret it, or
to assign a new importance to any known correspondence such as is
found in the latter part of this column. He will take the planetary rulers
here given as little more than suggestions for memorizing minor details
of the nature of the Zodiac. It would evidently be absurd to set up an
antinomy between the statement in this column that Saturn and Mercury
are the rulers of Libra with the statement elsewhere that Libra is ruled
by Venus and Saturn exalted therein. There is, however, a certain
partial sympathy between the columns. Thus Sol is exalted in Aries,
Luna in Taurus, Mercury rules Gemini, and Sol Leo. In the case of
Virgo, however, neither Venus nor Luna appear either as its ruler or as
exalted therein. A profitable meditation might develop in some such
way as follows:—

> *Question*: Why should Venus and Luna not be given as rulers of
> Virgo? Virgo is suggested as the Virgin Isis, Luna as
> sympathetic with solitude, purity and aptitude for reflection of
> the Hermit, ATU IX. Venus, again, as Binah, the recipient of
> Wisdom, represents one aspect of Virgo. So too does the earthy

nature of Venus in her aspect of Demeter. In this way an attribution, which at first sight is puzzling, may assist the student to harmonize many ideas which appear at first sight incompatible.

The case of Venus is germane to the argument (note that the symbol of Venus is the only planetary symbol which includes all ten Sephiroth). Venus is astrologically used as a synthetic term for the feminine aspect of the Deity. She then has many parts, Vesta, Ceres, Cybele, Isis, etc. The main distinction to be borne in mind is that with Luna; and the task is all the more difficult in that the symbols continually overlap. It is by harmonizing and transcending such difficulties that the student arrives at a metaphysical conception which is perfectly positive and lucid on the one hand, and on the other emancipated from the bondage of the Laws of Contradiction.

Luna = Gimel = 3. Trivia is one of the titles of Diana.

The ife of woman is naturally divided into three parts: before, during, and after the age of menstruation. (1) The Virgin, (2) the Wife and Mother, (3) the Hag. In (3) the woman can no longer fulfil her natural functions, which therefore turn to the malignity of despair. Hence the identification of the Hag with the Witch. (1) is represented by Diana, the virgin huntress (legends of Atalanta, Endymion, Pan, Actaeon, Persephone, etc.), Hebe, Pallas Athene, Pythia and the Sybils, etc. The function of the virgin is inspirational. (2) is connected with Venus, Ceres, Cyble, Kwannon or Kwanseon, Sekhet, Hathor, Kali, Aphrodite, Astarte, Ashtoreth, Artemis of the Ephesians, and many other female deities. (3) is a wholly malignant symbol. Hecaté and Nahema are the principal representatives of the idea.

Note that there are certain demons of the nature of Venus Aversa, symbolical of the evil caused by distorting or suppressing this principle. Such are Echidna, Lilith, the outraged Aphrodite for the Hyppolytus, the Venus of the Hørsel in Tannhäuser, Melusina, Lamia, some aspects of Kali, Kundry, possibly the malicious side of Queen Mad and the Fairy nature generally.

The student is expected to have in mind all such symbols and to overcome their incompatibility, not be blurring the outline of the different figures, but by regarding each of them as representing one phenomenal manifestation of the ultimate principle which we name Nuit, Teh, Shakti, Hé, Isis, positive electricity, the infinity of space, possibility, etc., in conjunction with a specific set of circumstances. The student will note that this principle cannot be apprehended in itself, but only in combination. Just so we can only understand electricity by observing its effects in lightning, magnetism, etc. Some philosophers have attempted to construct synthetic symbols to include all aspects of this principle. Thus the Egyptians, who were the most philosophical of all schools of Theogonists, included as many functions of femininity as possible in the idea of Isis. Thus she is:—

1. Wisdom, like Pallas Athene.
2. The Physical Moon.
3. The Perpetual Virgin, twice-born with Osiris.
4. Nature (compelemented by her final form Nephthys— Perfection).
5. The Builder of Cities. (As indicated by her head-dress).
6. The Spouse of Osiris.
7. The Mother of Horus.
8. The Spirit of Corn or food in general.
9. Earth in general.
10. The Goddess of Water or the Nile, and therefore of wine in general. She is the soul of intoxication, this represnting the spiritual rapture of physical love.
11. The Initiatrix; mistress of secrets. The Teacher.
12. The Restorer (the earth fertile after winter) as shown by her collecting the fragments of Osiris.

The feminine nature is evidently coextensive with a moiety of all our ideas; and this fact alone is sufficient to account for the complexity of the symbolism. Hence the necessity for a course of meditation above indicated and for the occasional apparent contradictions.

COLUMN XIII: THE PATHS OF THE SEPHER YETZIRAH

These attributions arise from the description of the paths in the Sepher Yetzirah. This is one of the most ancient books of the Qabalah; but it is far from clear how the ideas correspond with the general scheme of symbolism. They seem no use in practical magical work. It is doubtful whether the text of the book is accurate, or whether (in any case) the rabbin responsible for the text had sufficient authority.*

COLUMN XIV: GENERAL ATTRIBUTIONS OF THE TAROT

This column gives merely the actual attributions which are to be ataken as the basis of any investigation of the Tarot. They are the conventional terms and no more.

COLUMN XV: THE KING SCALE OF COLOUR

The four scales of colours (Columns XV–XVIII) are attributed to the four letters of Tetragrammaton. The King Scale represents the root of colour; that is, a relation is asserted between the essential significance of colour in the Atziluthic world, and that of the path understood as well as possible, in the light especially of Columns II, VI and XIV. But the King Sclae represents an essence of equal depth with the columns mentioned. It is an attribution of the same order as they; *i.e.* it is a primary expression of the essential ideas.

    1. Brilliance represents the colourless luminosity of Kether.

    2. The blue is that of the sky (Masloth).

    3. The crimson represents blood. Compare the symbolism of the Scarlet Woman and her Cup in Liber 418.

    4. The deep violet is episcopal. It combines 2 and 3, a bishop being the manifestation of heavenly or starry existence manifested through the principle of blood or animal life.

* [The text "The 32 Paths of Wisdom" from which the titles in Col. XIII were taken is not an intrinsic part of the *Sepher Yetzirah*, rather is believed to be a mediæval appendix to it. — T.S.]

5. The orange suggests the energy as opposed to other qualities of the Sun.

6. The rose is that of dawn. The attribution therefore asserts the identity of the Sun and Horus and is thus implicated with the doctrine of the New Æon.

7. Amber represents the electric voluptuousness of Aphrodite. It suggests the tint of the skin of those women who are most enthusiastically consecrated to Venus.

8. Violet-purple. Should this not be lavender? Meditate.

9. The indigo is that of the Akasa (ether) and of the throat of Shiva. It represents the night sky blue of the nemyss of Thoth. This nemyss is the mysterious yet pregnant darkness which surrounds the generative process.

10. The yellow indicates Malkuth as the appearance which our senses attach to the solar radiance. In other words, Malkuth is the illusion which we make in order to represent to ourselves the energy of the universe.

THE ELEMENTAL COLOURS

These may be naturally derived from what has been said about Column XI, lines 1-10. Scarlet naturally represents the activity of Fire, blue the passivity of Water, while yellow is the balance between them. Green is the middle colour of the spectrum and therefore the balanced receptacle of the totality of vibration. Observe that the complementary of each of the pair of the colours of the active elements is the third. Thus red and blue make violet, whose complementary is yellow; and so on.

For the citrine, olive, russet, and black of earth, see the explanation under 10, Malkuth, in the Queen Scale (Column XVI). The pure earth, known to the ancient Egyptians in that Equinox of the Gods over which Isis presided, was green.

THE PLANETARY ATTRIBUTIONS

They follow the colours of the spectrum. They are the transparent as opposed to the reflected colours. They follow the order of the subtlety and spirituality of the vibration. Thus the violet of Jupiter is definitely religious and creative, which at the end of the scale the red of Mars is physical, violent and gross. Between these we have Saturn whose indigo represents the sobriety and deep-sea calmness of meditation, Saturn being the eldest of the Gods. Luna is blue; representing purity, aspiration and unselfish love. The green of Venus suggests the vibration of vegetable growth. It is the intermediate stage between the definitely spiritual and the definitely intellectual and emotional type of vibration. In the "rods and cones" attribution green is the central colour, the pure passivity absorbing all: as Venus combines all the Sephiroth in one symbol. The yellow of Mercury suggests the balanced but articulate movement of the mind. The orange of Sol is the intense but gross physical vibration of animal life.

The above represents merely one of an indefinitely large number of interpretations which may be derived from meditation on this attribution.

THE ZODIACAL ATTRIBUTIONS

The Zodiacal colours proceed systematically from the Scarlet of Aries to the violet of Aquarius. The colour which completes the circle is described as crimson, and is attributed to Pisces, the allusion being to the relation of Pisces with Binah through the ATU XVIII, the Moon, in which also is shown the pool of midnight through which Kephra travels in his bark; and this suggests the Night of Pan which hangs over the City of the Pyramids. Aries is scarlet, being the House of Mars and the sign of the Spring Equinox, where occurs the fiery outburst of the new year. Taurus is red-orange, suggesting the red earth of which man (who is Taurus, Vau, Microprosopus, the Son) is made, the orange indicating the Solar influence and the energy of Geburah. Gemini is orange, since ATU VI shows the Solar twins Vau Hé. Cancer is amber, the connection being with Netzach, Venus in her less spiritual form being the chariot or vehicle through which the influence of the Supernal Mother is conveys to man. In this chariot is borne the Sangraal or Cup of Babalon which connects the symbolism with the legend of Parsifal and the visions of Liber 418. The ideas of love and electricity are implicit in this sign, which is ruled by the Moon and in which Jupiter is exalted.

Leo is pure yellow, yet with that tinge of green which is characteristic of the purest gold. It suggests the first form of the principle of vegetable growth, implicit in the nature of the Solar ray.

Virgo has the yellowish green of young grass. The connection is evident.

Libra is emerald green, being pre-eminently the house of Venus.

Scorpio is the greenish blue—Prussian blue—whose psychological effect upon the sensitive mind is to suggest a poisonous or putrafactive vibration. It contains the idea of life and death interpenetrating each other and reproducing each other continuously; always with the accompaniment of a certain morbid pleasure. It is the identification which one finds in Swinburne's best poems: "The Garden of Proserpine," "Dolores," "Illicet," "Anactoria," and others. The natural correspondence is the blue-green sea.*

Sagittarius is blue; being the House of Jupiter, which is blue in the Queen Scale. It is also the blue of the sky, for Sagittarius is the background of the Rainbow symbolism of Q Sh Th. It is further connected with the blue of religious aspiration. It continues the path of Gimel. It is the aspiration from Yesod to Tiphereth as Gimel is from Tiphereth to Kether. Note that the aspiration from Malkuth is *dark* blue: it being so low on the Tree its purity is to some extent darkned.

Capricornus is indigo. The connection is with the colour of Yesod, implying the sexual symbolism of the Goat.

Aquarius is violet: this is connected with ATU XVII. Cf. *The Book of the Law*, I, 61-64. The colour violet, generally speaking, signifies a vibration which is at the same time spiritual and erotic; *i.e.* it is the most intense of the vibrations alike on the planes of Nephesch and Neschamah. Compare at the other end of the scale the connection between the vibrations of Mars and those of the Sangraal.

---

* [One of Swinburne's favourite sources of metaphors. — T.S.]

COLUMN XVI: THE QUEEN SCALE

This scale represents the first positive appearance of colour: as the King Scale is transparent, the Queen is reflected. (Spectra.)

1-3. In this scale, therefore, we read the appearance of the 32 paths as they are found in Nature. Kether, being previously unconditioned brilliance, is now articulate as white. The grey of Chokmah refers to the cloudy appearance of semen, and indicates the transmission of white to black. It is the double nature of the Dyad. Binah is black, having the faculty of absorbing all colours. In the three Supernals, therefore, we find the 3 possible modifications of light, in its wholeness. Above the abyss there is no separation into colour.

4. Chesed has the blue of water
5. Geburah has the red of fire.
6. Tiphereth the yellow of air.

(These being the 3 primary colours of reflected light, as opposed to the violet, green and blue of transparent light.)

The colours of the 3rd triad are derived from those of the 2nd by simple admixture.

7. Netzach. Emerald is Chesed and Tiphereth mingled. It is also the colour of Venus.

8. Hod. Orange is Tiphereth and Geburah mingled.

9. Yesod. Violet is Chesed and Geburah mingled

Netzach and Hod are naturally the resultant of the two Sephiroth which impinge on them respecitvely, while Yesod represents a secondary effect of the conjunction of Geburah and Chesed, Tiphereth being the primary. Emerald represents the most brilliant aspect of Venus; orange that of Mercury. Violet of the very complex formula synthesizes Yesod in the idea of Luna. Note that Sol and Luna are direct images of the masculine and feminine principles, and much more complete Macrocosms than any other planets. This is explained by their symbols in the Yi King, ☰ and ☷. Note also that Yesod appears openly, this being the Queen Scale, in the violet robes of the spiritual-erotic vibrations referred to above.

10. Malkuth. Just as the third Triad combines the colours of the second Triad by pairs, so does Malkuth in a yet more complete manner. Citrine combines blue, red and yellow with a predominance of yellow; olive, with a predominance of blue; ruesset, with a predominance of red; and these represent respectively the airy, watery, and fiery sub-elements. Black is the earthy part of Earth. But here we observe a phenomenon compatible with that found in the Tarot, where the four Empresses (symbolical of Hé final) are the throne of the Spirit as well as being the ultimate recipients of the force of King, Queen, and Emperor. The black is the link between the lowest conception, the climax of the degeneration of pure colour in the final assimilation of light, and the black of Binah. It is the lowest part of the daughter which contains in darkness the identity with the Pure Mother, to set her upon whose throne is one definite image of the Great Work. See also the 27th Symbol in Liber XXVII;* the ultimate of the feminine symbols, the complete dissociation of existence, the final disappearance of all positive ideas, but this is found to be essentially identical with the perfection of the continuum.†

The planetary colours are connected chiefly with the sacred metals as observed clairvoyantly, or considered in respect of their astrological and alchemical character. Mercury is purple suggesting the iridescence of quicksilver and the blue of Mercury vapour. Luna is silver, the apparent colour of the Moon in the sky, and of the metal to which she is attributed. Venus is sky-blue; this is possibly a reference to copper sulphate, an important salt in alchemy; but principally because sky-blue naturally suggests the more frivolous aspects of love. The blue of Jupiter refers to the blue of the sky, his dominion, and to the appropriate colour of religious aspiration. Mars is red on account of the colour of

---

* ["☷ Therefore was the end of it sorrow; yet in that sorrow a sixfold star of glory whereby they might see to return unto the stainless Abode; yea, unto the Stainless Abode."]

† [No explanation of the elemental colours of the Queen scale appeared in the printed edition. At least part of the reference, though, seems to be to the corresponding Tattwa symbol: see Col. LXXV in the main table. — T.S.]

rust, and of the use of iron in executing the pure will; whether by sword, spear or machine. Sol is yellow, the apparent colour of the sun, and of the metal gold. Saturn is black with reference to Binah, the sphere of Saturn, to the Night of Pan (see Liber 418 in *Equinox* I, 5), to the blackness of oblivion (Saturn being Time), and to the blackness of the Tamoguna, Saturn representing the inactivity of old age.

Zodiacal colours are less obvious in their attribution. In fact it will be best to take this part of the column for what it may be worth as an uninitiated tradition. I am myself unable to attach any serious and important meaning to the majority of the symbols. At most, one can say that the colour of the scale represennts the degeneration of the Key Scale. *E.g.* in the case of Aries, red represents a mere dulling of the previous scarlet. The deep indigo of Taurus suggests the laborious sadness of the brute part of man; the slate-green of Virgo may refer to the apparent ennui or colourless melancholy of the hermit life. The black of Capricorn refers to the popular idea of ATU XV; while the attribution of Pisces may refer to the actual appearance of some fish, or to certain phenomena characteristic of the astral plane.

COLUMN XVII: THE EMPEROR SCALE

The scale of the Emperor is derived from the two previous scales by simple admixture, as of colours on a palette for the most part.

COLUMN XVIII: THE EMPRESS SCALE

The scale of the Empress is, generally speaking, either a degeneration from the scale of the Emperor or a complementary attribution, Hé being the twin of Vau. But in each case there is an added brightness whose source must be discovered by meditation. This brightness is a phenomenon compatible to that described above in connection with the Empresses being the thrones of the Spirit, and Malkuth being the extreme departure from the perfection of the Supernals, and so the link through which the redemption of the whole complex substructure below the Abyss may be accomplished.

The colours of the Empress Scale are combinations of two or more colours. The best may be considered as derived from the three previous scales, and the flecks or rays as representative of the bridegroom who is appointed to bring the Empress to perfection thus.

1. White flecked gold. The white is a reflection of the white brilliance of Kether; but the gold is an ornament, and thus indicates the mystery of the Holy Guardian Angel, who finds added perfection when invoked by his client, the gold of Tiphereth.

2. Red, blue, and yellow are the results of the creative energy of Chokmah and their white basis signifies that Chokmah has been perfected by fulfilling his function in this way. Also, the robe of the perfected Osiris is white flecked with red, blue, and yellow.

3. As the grey of Chokmah was perfected to the white of Kether, so the black of Binah is perfected to the grey of Chokmah. The grey is flecked with the pink of Tiphereth. This is the dawn of the child with which she is heavy, for this is the symbol of her perfection.

4. Deep azure represents Jupiter and Water. It is flecked with yellow. This represents religious meditation; the yellow flecks are the first marks of ecstasy.

5. Red is the most passive shade of the scarlet of the two former scales. The black flecks show that in its perfection it receives the influence of Binah, the Supernal immediately above it in the Tree.

6. Gold amber suggests the mellowness of harvest, which is the perfection of the rose-pink of dawn, the spring of the day.

7. There seems a possible reference to Semele; and the general idea is that Netzach has been brought to a quiet harmonious tone and is receiving the influence of Tiphereth. Olive flecked gold.

8. This is a mystery of Mercury, improper to indicate clearly.* Yellowish brown flecked white.

9. Citrine represents the final modification of Yesod, the airy nature at last appearing. The azure flecks are derived from Chesed—perhaps through Netzach; or from Sagittarius, the path joining it with Tiphereth.

---

* [A hint may perhaps be found in Liber 415, "Opus Lutetianum." — T.S.]

10. Malkuth has been set upon the throne of Binah; and the rays of the bridgegroom Tiphereth flood her with Gold. Blakc rayed yellow.

THE ELEMENTS

11. Air has been made fertile, so that the golden flecks of the Sun are able to illumine it. Air is naturally barren. The green represents the Lotus on which Harpocrates is seated, or from which he is born.

23. The perfection of Water is indicated by its iridescence. This is the alchemical symbolism.

31. Fire, being pure, retains its original vermillion; but it has become capable of being the home of the crimson and emeral of Binah and her sphere of joy, Venus. It is no longer a destructive element, but the proper abode of Love, both in its higher and lower forms.

32 bis. Earth is identical with Malkuth, save that the rays are now flecks. The symbolism is similar.

31 bis. Spirit manifests the scale of five colours as shown on the Uræus Wand. (*The Equinox* I (3), p. 211.)* Its perfection is to complete itself in the Pentagram. The mystery is similar to that mentioned in connection with 1 above.

THE PLANETS

12. *Mercury's* perfection is to still and concentrate thought, until it becomes deep red through which runs the violet vibration of spiritual-erotic ecstasy. (Note that the great defect of Mercury is its cold-bloodedness).

13. *Luna.* The original chastity of the Moon is tinged with Love.

14. *Venus.* The defect of Venus is its tendency to romance (rose or cerise)—"External Splendour" Nogah. It is perfected by reality and usefulness—the emerald of vegetable life and growth.

21. *Jupiter.* The religious devotion of Jupiter is rewarded by the yellow rays of the Holy Guardian Angel.

27. *Mars.* The energy of Mars has been subdued until it is a proper bases for the blue and green rays of vegetable and spiritual life. (Cf.

* [The reference is to the wand of the Chief Adept in the Adeptus Minor ritual of the R.R. et A.C. It is topped by a winged globe with two Uræus serpents descending from it, the shaft is coloured white, red, blue, yellow and black for the Elements. — T.S.]

under "31. Fire," above.)

30. *Sol.* The perfection of Sol is its fixation in the amber of Cancer by elevation at the summer solstice. In this it receives the adornment of pure physical energy, Fire. The red is purer than the orange, being of the incorruptible element.

32. *Saturn.* The perfection of Saturn is its identification with Binah. It has, so to speak, made good its position above the Abyss. It is adorned with the blue rays of the King Scale of Chokmah. The symbol implies that Time, the Destroyer, has been transmuted into the condition of the operation of the Great Work, *i.e.* the marriage of Chokmah and Binah.

THE ZODIAC

15. *Aries.* Controlled fire as in a furnace.

16. *Taurus.* Rich fertile earth.

17. *Gemini* is perfected by active thoughts, aimed and tinged by spiritual intention.

18. *Cancer.* See Liber 418 (*Equinox* I, 5) on the Mysteries of Magister Templi. The blood in the Cup of Babalon has dried to brown in which the vegetable, impersonal, and immortal life lurks.

19. *Leo.* Fire is infused evenly in the Lion, thus correcting his tendency to impulse.

20. *Virgo.* The perfection of virginity is fruitfulness.

22. *Libra.* Retains the love of its ruler Venus, but this is purified of its grossness.

22. *Scorpio.* The vivid watery vibration of putrefaction assumes the hue of the beetle Kephra. The perfection of Scorpio is to bring corruptibility through its midnight.

25. *Sagittarius.* The virgin huntress is brought from her superficiality by becoming the huntress Babalon. The deep vivid blue is to be connected with the ideas of water (the Great Sea of Binah) and Chesed, the image of that sea below the Abyss.

26. *Capricornus.* The colour combines Chokmah and Binah, and is very dark. The Great Attainment is symbolized by the marriage.

28. *Aquarius* is the Kerub of the Man; and his perfection is to attain the purity of Kether (white) tinged with the purple or violet vibrations explained above.

29. *Pisces* is the symbol of the Astral Plane. (See ATU XVIII.) Its defect is glamour and illusion. It has now been brought to a mental equilibrium signifying the adaptability of the ether to receive and transmit all types of vibration.

MINUTUM MUNDUM

A General Note on Columns XV-XVIII, the Four Scales of Colour

You can use the four scales of colour as you choose. The only thing to remember is the attribution, the Tetragrammaton.

The Sephiroth are given in the King's Scale and the paths in the Queen's Scale* in accordance with the general law of balance. You must never have a masculine sticking out by itself without a feminine to equilibrate it.

The Sephiroth are definitely positve ideas. The numbers are "Things in Themselves," much more so that the letters of the alphabet. The paths are merely the links between the Sephiroth.

Of course the idea of balance is carried into the Sephiroth themselves. The number 4 is masculine in its relation with number 5, feminine in its relation with number 3.

You cannot go wrong as long as you keep always this idea of balance in the forefront of your mind. Whenever one thing goes on to another thing, there must always be this opposition, and equilibrium. You can apply this to every point that comes up in practical working. It is always possible to refer any system of symbols to the Tree of Life merely by Tetragrammaton, or indeed to any of the fundamental systems of classification. It is a very useful exercise to practice this type of analysis. Take, for example, the letter Daleth, and note all is correspondences. For instance, you get at once the equation $4 = 7$, for the numerical of Daleth is 4, while 7 is of Venus.

* [The other way round is more usual. — T.S.]

The more thoroughly you practice this the nearer you will come to the completely automatic subconscious understanding of the essence of any given symbol.

COLUMNS XIX, XX, XXI, XXXIV, XXXV: GENERAL REMARKS ON THE GODS

Many of the so-called names of God, such as the 99 names of Allah and the poetical lists of Hinduism, are not really names at all but descriptive titles. By the true name of a God we mean that word which represents his Magical Formula: the due process of which therefore sets his energy in motion. (See J.G. Frazer for numerous legends illustrating this idea.)* There cannot therefore be more true names ultimately than distinct sounds. For a God with a compound name would represent a complex sound, and therefore a complex energy. Such a God would lack the simplicity which is the first attribute of Godhead.

Outside the Hebrew and such other names of Gods as can be checked and corrected if necessary by the rules of Gematria, or the Yetziratic or Tarotic attribution, there is no adequate security that corruption has not taken place, *e.g.* Osiris instead of Asar; Jupiter instead of IAO-Pater.

There are numerous dialectic changes, and changes due to corruption in the course of time or to deliberate modification, with such ends in view as the identification of a local deity with an important and popular God of similar name.

The uncertainty of primitive alphabets is responsible for mispronunciations, which are then written down phonetically and again mispronounced, so that in course of time one finds a form which cannot be recognised; *e.g.* confusion has arisen from the writing of the sound S with a C, pronouncing the C hard and then (to avoid mistakes!) replacing it by K. There is also confusion between I or Y and J (Dj), soft G and hard G, so that a name originally pronounced with a Y ends by appearing with a hard G.

---

* [*Taboo and the Perils of the Soul*, cap. VI § 5.]

The popularity of a Deity lends to his or her identification with the local interests of each new groups of worshippers. Thus a corn goddess might appeal, for one reason or another, to town-dwellers, who would then acclaim her as especially protectress of cities. The process in its widest possibilities is practically universal in the case of those divinities whose cult covers any considerable variety of climates, cultures, economic and social conditions and centuries. Thus a primitive God may be worshipped under a corruption of his original name, and also by his original character. The evolution of Gods proceeds *pari passu* with that of their devotees.

From this it will be clear that except in the case of the Hebrews and of a few isolated instances, it is almost impossible to decide on a satisfactory attribution for any given name. It is only when the cult of the god is limited so that his symbolic form, attributes and legend have some single or at least predominant characteristic, that one can make use even of correctness, much less of completeness. Such is Sekhet, who is uniformly represented with a lion's head and described as possessing feline qualities, so that we can assign her to Leo without hesitation. But a goddess like Isis might be given to Zero as co-terminous with Nature, to 3 as Mother, to 4 as Venus, to 6 as Harmony, to 7 as Love, to 8 as the Moon, to 10 as Virgin, to 13 again as the Moon, to 14 as Venus, to 15 as connected with the letter Hé, to 16 as the Sacred Cow, to 18 as Goddess of Water, to 24 as Draco, to 28 as Giver of Rain, to 29 as the Moon, and to 32 as Lady of the Mysteries (Saturn, Binah). In such cases one must be content with a more or less arbitrary selection, and make an independent investigation in each particular case in reference to the matter immediately under consideration. The complementary confusion is that Deities of very different nature will appear against the same rank of the Key Scale for different reasons. For instance, the number 4 includes both Isis and Amoun. There is no question of identifying these. The fact of their appearing in the same place must be taken to indicate that both ideas are necessary to complete the connotation of the number 4.

COLUMN XIX: SOME EGYPTIAN GODS

0. Against the number Zero Harpocrates is Silence and Rest, Amoun is the Concealed. For Nuit and Hadit see the Commentary to the *Book of the Law*.

1. Now in the number 1, Ptah is the Creator, being represented as a mummy without gestures. It signifies that Kether has no attributes. Asar-un-Nefer is the perfected Osiris; that is Osiris brought to Kether. Heru-Ra-Ha contains the twin forms of the Lord of Æon. He is Kether to use in this time and place as being the highest positive conception of which we are capable.

2. Amoun as the creative Chiah, Thoth as the Logos, Nuit as connected with Mazloth.

3. Maut the Mother Vulture requiring to be impregnated by Air, the Logos. Isis as the Mother. Nephthys as the Mother in her dark aspect.

4. Amoun as the Father; Isis as water, and Hathoor the Nile Goddess.

5. Horus as the Lord of Force. Nephthys as the Lady of Severity balancing the Mercy of Isis.

6. Asar, the prototype of man. Ra and On the Sun God. Harpocrates is of Tiphereth as being the Child. Also he is the centre, as Tiphereth is the centre of the Ruach. His body is rose-pink, as in the King Scale of Tiphereth. Hrumachis might also be places her for the same reason.

7. Hathoor, the Egyptian Venus.

8. Anubis, the lower form of Thoth, Mercury.

9. Shu, Lord of the Firmament, supporting it as Yesod supports the Sephiroth 4–8 of the Tree of Life. Hermanubis, the Lord of the Threshold, because he is Yesod, the link between Ruach and Nephesch. All exclusively phallic Gods might be attributed here.

10. Seb as the Lord of Earth. The lower Isis and Nephthys as Virgins, imperfect until impregnated. Sphinx, as containing the 4 Elements or Kerubs.

THE ELEMENTS

11. Nu is the Lord of the Firmament, Hoor-pa-kraat is the Fool of the Tarot. Air.

23. Tum as the Sun descending into ocean. Ptah as the Mummy. Compare ATU XII. Auramoth, Goddess of Water. Asar as ATU XII. Isis as Goddess of Water. Hathoor as Goddess of Pleasure. Water.

31. Thoum-aesh-neither, Goddess of Fire. Mau the Lion—Sun in the South. Kabeshunt—Kerub of Fire. Horus, God of Fire.

32 bis. Ahapshi, Kerub of Earth. Nephthys, Goddess of Earth as Isis is of Water. Ameshet, Kerub of Earth.

31 bis. Asar represents Spirit as being the ideal God in the normal man.

THE PLANETS

12. Thoth and Cynocephalos, Mercurial gods.

13. Chomse, God of the Moon.

14. Hathoor, Goddess of Love.

21. Amoun-Ra, Jupiter as Creator.

27. Horus as Warrior God.

30. Sun gods.

32. Crocodile gods, devourers.

THE ZODIAC

15. Men Thu as a martial God.

16. Asar as the Redeemer. Ameshet as Kerub of Earth. Apis as Bull.

17. Twin deities as pertaining to Gemini. Heru-Ra-Ha as containing the twin Horus Deities.

18. Kephra perhaps, because Cancer is in the nadir in the horoscope when Aries is rising.

19. Babalon and the Beast conjoined. Refers to ATU XI. Pasht, Sekhet and Mau are all Lions.

20. Isis is the Virgin.

22. Ma, Goddess of Truth and Justice (ATU VIII).

24. These are all Serpent or Dragon deities. Typhon espeically Lord of destruction and death.

25. Nephthys. Perfection presides over Transmutation.

26. Khem is the erect Phallus. Set, see ATU XV. Capricornus is the House of the Sun at the extreme southern declination.

28. Ahepi, Kerub of Air.

29. See ATU XVIII.

COLUMN XXI: THE PERFECTED MAN

These attributions all refer to those parts of the human body on the Tree of Life.

COLUMN XXII: SOME HINDU DEITIES

Add the following: 1. Shiva, Brahma. 7. Bhaviani, etc. 18. Krishna. 24. Yama. 27. Krishna. 28. The Maruts.

COLUMN XXXIV: SOME GREEK GODS

0. Pan is the All which is o. He has the power of destroying all positive manifestation.

1. Zeus is the Supreme Unity, not to be confused with the Zeus who is the son of Kronos. Iacchus is the supreme unity in man reached by ecstasy, when everything else has been winnowed away by the winnowing fan.

2. Athena as the Wisdom which springs full-armed from the brain of Zeus. Uranus as the Starry Heaven, Hermes as the Messenger or Logos.

3. The Goddesses are all Mothers. Psyche is the Neschamah. Kronos is Saturn, the dark one and the limiation of Time.

4. Poseidon, Lord of Water. Zeus, the All-Father.

5. Ares, Lord of War. Hades, God of Fire in the partition between him and Zeus and Poseidon.

6. Iacchus as the Holy Guardian Angel. Apollo as the God of the Sun and male beauty. Adonis, the dying-God. Dionysus and Bacchus as different aspects of this God.

7. Aphrodite, Goddess of Love. Niké, Goddess of Victory. Netzach.

8. Hermes, Mercurial.

9. Zeus, equals Shu, God of Air. Diana as phallic stone and Luna. Eros as representing the reproductive passion.

10. Persephone, the virgin Earth. See her legend. She is Malkuth of Demeter and Binah. Adonis is a doubtful attribution, the connection being with Adonai as God of Earth. Psyche the unredeemed Soul. Compare line 3 above.

THE ELEMENTS

11. Zeus, God of Air.

23. Poseidon, God of Water.

31. Hades, God of Fire.

32 bis. Demeter, Goddess of Corn. Gaia, Earth itself.

31 bis. Iacchus, Spirit. Compare line 1 above.

THE PLANETS

12. Hermes, Mercurial.

13. Artemis, the virgin Moon. Hecate, the evil Moon.

14. These are all Deities of Love.

21. Zeus as Jupiter.

27. Ares, God of War, and Athene the Warrior Goddess.

30. Sun Gods.

32. Athene as the Higher Wisdom. Might also be attributed to Line 3. Kronos as Saturn.

THE ZODIAC

15. Athena pertaining to the head.

16. Heré: a doubtful attribution but there may be some connection with the Heavenly Cow.*

17. Castor and Pollux as Twins. Apollo was the inspirer of Oracles. Eros might be added if the topmost figure in ATU VI really represents him.

18. Apollo as the Charioteer.

* [In the printed edition the above entries for 15 and 16 were corrupted and combined into one under Line 16, reading: "Athena pertaining to the head. Here a doubtful attribution..." Heré may be 'Ηρη, the Ionic spelling of 'Ηρα, Hera. — T.S.]

19. Demeter borne by lions.

20. Attis. He is of course a dying-God but is attributed here because of his mutilation which corresponds to Virgo.*

22. Themis, Goddess of Justice.

24. Ares, because Mars rules Scorpio. Apollo the Pythean because of his Serpent. Thanatos because of ATU XIII.

25. These attributions made because Sagittarius is a hunting Sign.

26. Capricornus: these attributions refer to the erect phallus.

28. Ganymede, the Cup-bearer, is referred to the Water-carrier.

29. Poseidon, because of the watery nature of Pisces. Hermes psychopompos, connected with the symbolism of Kephra travelling under the earth.

COLUMN XXXV: SOME ROMAN GODS

0. The Latin Spirit does not admit other than positive ideas.

1. Jupiter as the Supreme Creator.

2. Janus is the Dyad. Mercury as the Mesenger.

3. These attributions are given because of their dark lunar, limited, or maternal character.

4. Jupiter is the Father. Libitina is connected with the amniotic fluid.

5. Mars, the War God.

6. Apollo, the Sun God. Bacchus, the inspirer of Harmony and Beauty; also called Aurora, Goddess of Dawn, rose-pink of Tiphereth.

7. Venus, Goddess of Love (Ananda).†

8. Mercury, God of Thought (Chit).†

9. Diana, Goddess of the Moon. Terminus, marking the boundary. Compare Hermanubis. Jupiter as God of Air and as the foundation (Sat).†

10. Ceres, Goddess of Earth.

THE ELEMENTS

11. Jupiter, Lord of Air. Bacchus connected with ATU 0. Juno, Goddess of Air. Æolus, God of the Winds.

---

* [See Frazer, *Adonis Attis Osiris*. — T.S.]
† See "The Naples Arrangement," p. 36.

23. Neptune, God of Water. Rhea, Goddess who flows.

31. These are Gods of Fire.

32 bis. Ceres, Goddess of Earth.

31 bis. Bacchus, as Lord of Ecstasy. Spirit.

THE PLANETS

These attributions are all obvious. It is, in fact, largely on the mythological and astrological conception of these Gods and Goddesses that the intelligibility of this whole Table is based. They represent the fundamental familiar ideas.

30. Ops, God of Wealth, which is solar.

32. Terminus, because Saturn is the end of things. Astræa is attributed here in so far as she may be taken to represent the central figure in ATU XXI.

THE ZODIAC

15. Mars, ruler of Aries. Minerva as for Athena in Column XXXIV.

16. Venus, Lady of Taurus. Hymen is given here because of its connection with ATU V. See Catullus, Pervigillium Veneris.

17. Twin Gods. Hymen as relating to ATU VI.

18. Mercury is here attributed because the path of Cancer leads from the Supernal Binah to Geburah. This is a reference to ATU VII. But this attribution is very doubtful. The bearer of the Graal is not Hermes the Mesenger. The Lares and Penates are given as Gods of the Home, Cancer being the sign of receptivity and settlement; but again this attribution is not altogether satisfactory.

19. ATU XI may be regarded as representing the Fire of Vulcan.

20. Vesta, the Virgin Goddess. Ceres, Flora and Adonis are given here because of their connection with spring, which is suggested by the yellowish-green colour in the King Scale.

22. A Goddess of Justice might be attributed here but in the higher sense of the Eighth ATU, the main idea is that of the satisfied woman; we might therefore insert Venus which rules Libra. Note that Saturn is exalted in Libra. Nemesis represents the ultimate automatic justice of Nature. ATU VIII may have some connection with the awakening of

the Eld of the All-Father. See Liber 418 in *The Equinox*, I, 5.

24. Mars, as Ruler of Scorpio. Mors, because of ATU XIII.

25. Diana, as bearing bow and arrows. Iris, because of the rainbow.

26. Vesta is here attributed because of Capricorn being the secret flame. The other gods refer to the erect phallus.

28. Juno, Lady of Air. Æolus, God of the Winds. The month of February, when the Sun is in Aquarius, was traditionally sacred to Juno.

29. Neptune, because Pisces is a watery sign.

COLUMN XXXVIII: ANIMALS, REAL AND IMAGINARY

o. The Dragon represents Draco connected with Nuit in the Heaven; Ananta, the great serpent which surrounds the Universe. It devours its own tail, thereby reducing it to Zero.

1. The Swan as representing Aum. See Liber LXV, Cap. II, 17-25. See also *The Book of Lies*, Cap. XVII. The Hawk pertains to Kether, as poised in the ether and beholding all things. Remember that Kether is primarily the individual point of view. The Soul beholds all things and changes the place according to its going. Thus in the Egyptian tradition the Hawk is the symbol of the highest type of Godhead.

3. The Bee is the traditional attribution of the Yoni.

4. Again, traditional. It is probably connected with the erect phallus of Amoun. The Unicorn is also Jupiterean, as connected with the horse of Sagittarius.

5. The Basilisk represents Geburah on account of its power of slaying with the flame of its glance.

6. The Phoenix on account of its symbolism of the $5°=6°$ grade. Lion, as the typical animal of Sol. Child, as Vau of Tetragrammaton. The Spider is particularly sacred to Tiphereth. It is written that she "taketh hold with her hands and is in kings' palaces."* (The most characteristic title of Tiphereth is the "Palace of the King.") She has six legs† and is in the centre of her web exactly as Tiphereth is in the centre

---

* [Proverbs, XXX. 28.]

† [Only because you've pulled two off, Aleister. On the Kircher Tree of Life, there are eight paths radiating from Tiphareth. — T.S.]

of the Sephiroth of Ruach. The Pelican represents the Redeemer feeding its children with its own blood, and for this reason it has been chosen as the special symbol of the Brethren of the R & C.

7. Iynx. This attribution is traditional. See Eliphas Levi's design of the pantomorphous Iynx.* The Raven pertains to Netzach because of the qliphotic attribution in Column VIII. All carrion birds may be attributed here, because of their connection with Victory. Note that the path of Scorpio connects Tiphereth with Netzach. The idea of Venus is intimately connected with that of death, for death is in many important senses a part of love. Compare the *Book of Lies*, Caps. I, VIII, XV, XVI, and XVIII, etc., etc.

8. Hermaphrodite, as representing the dual nature of Mercury. Jackal, sacred to Anubis. Twin serpents. These represent the Mercurial double current as on the Caduceus. See the interpretation given in the Paris Working. Monokeros de Astris.† This animal is given as the symbolical title of a Practicus. It is the swiftness of his motion which chielfy warrants the attributions. See Liber LXV, Cap. III, v. 2. He seems to combine the masculine and feminine element: on the one hand, the horn and the speed symbolism, on the other his white colour, his silver collar, and its inscription, *linea viridis gyrat universa*,‡ which

* [Iynx: *Grk.*, Ιυνξ (pl. Ιυγγες), the wryneck: a bird of the woodpecker family which had the misfortune to be used in early Greek love-magick (hence the attribution); but in the *Chaldæan Oracles* the Iunges appear to have been a group of ministering powers who stood between the theurgist and the Supreme God (see Lewy, *Chaldæan Oracles and Theurgy*), whence they are cited in the ritual of the Star Ruby. It does not rhyme with "sphinx." Lévi's figure of the "pantamorphous Iynx" appears as a plate to his *Histoire de la Magie* and appears to be an Egyptian goddess, possibly a form of Isis-Hathor. — T.S.]
† [Approx., "Unicorn from the Stars."]
‡ [Lat., "the green line encircles the Universe." Quoted by Giovanni Pico della Mirandola as a Cabalistic aphorism in his *Conclusiones*: "cum dicit Salamon in oratione suo in Libro Regnum: Exaudi, o cœlum, per cœlum lineam viridem debemus intelligere quæ gyrat universam" (When Solomon says, in his prayer in the Book of Kings, Hear, o heaven, by heaven we must understand the green line which encircles the universe). There may be a reference to the Dragon Theli spoken of in the *Sepher Yetzirah*. As Crowley notes elsewhere, the planetary symbol for Venus is the only one which can be plotted on the Kircher Tree of Life without stretching or rearranging the

refers to Venus as containing the Universe.

9. Elephant, sacred to Ganesha, the god who breaks down obstacles. Hence placed in Yesod for the same reason as Anubis. Tortoise, as supporting the Elephant, hence equivalent to Atlas. Toad, "ugly and venomous, wears yet a precious jewel in his head." This refers to his generative force.

10. The Sphinx as containing the 4th Element, the Child, Hé final, twin of the male child Vau.

THE ELEMENTS

21. The Eagle, king of the birds. Man as the Kerub of Air. Ox—actual meaning of Aleph.

23. The Eagle-Snake-Scorpion trinity is the Kerub of Water.

31. The Lion is the Kerub of Fire.

32 bis. The Bull is the Kerub of Earth.

THE PLANETS

12. The Swallow for its swiftness. The Ibis, sacred to Thoth; the Ape, sacred to Thoth. The Cynocephalos is the constant companion of Thoth and produces base imitations of his Wisdom and Power. The Twin Serpents for the same reason as in line 8. All fish are sacred to Mercury because of their swiftness, their cold-bloodedness, the gleaming white or iridescent colours which are characteristic of their scales, and to some extent to their method of reproduction. Hybrids may also be attributed here, as to line 17.

13. The Dog, as baying at the Moon and the natural companion of the huntress Artemis. The white Stork, perhaps as traditionally announcing childbirth. The Camel as the actual meaning of the letter. It conveys travellers across the desert as the path of Gimel crosses the Abyss from Tiphereth to Kether. See also *Book of Lies*, Cap. XLII.

14. The Sparrow and Dove are especially sacred to Venus. See Catullus's Ode to Lesbia,* *Tristram Shandy*, Sappho's Ode to Venus, *etc.* For the Dove see Martial's ode referring to Catullus' Sparrow, the

---

figure in such a way that it includes all ten Sephiroth (circle centred on Da'ath going through 1-6, cross formed from the paths of Samekh, Pé and Tau joining 7-10). — T.S.]

* [The reference is probably to poem II in the standard edition of Catullus. — T.S.]

legend of the Virgin Mary, *etc.* The Dove is also Venusian on account of its soft amiability. The Swan, for the same reason as above. The Sow, the female of the boar of Mars; also because the sensuality of the sow suggests the lower type of Venus. All birds are primarily sacred to Venus, probably because the instinct of love enables a man to rise for a sime above the earth. Also because of their great beauty of form and colour, because their flesh is tender as compared to that of aniamls, and because there speech is of the nature of ecstatic song and is devoid of any intellectual quality.

21. The Eagle is the sacred bird of Jupiter. The Praying Mantis suggests Jupiter by its simulation of a devotional attitude.

27. The Horse is sacred to Mars chiefly on account of his spirited nature. The Bear is martial chiefly for alchemical reasons and because of his great strength. The Wolf is sacred to Mars (see the legend of Rome), also on account of his savage nature. The Boar is martial, as shown in the legend of Adonis. There is here a mystery of the grade of 6°=5□, the overawing of Tiphereth by Geburah.

30. The Lion is the typically solar animal. The Hawk is solar as all-seeing. The Leopard is sacred to the sun on account of its black spots.

31. The Crocodile is Saturnian, as the devourer.

THE ZODIAC

15. The Ram is Aries by meaning. The attribution refers to his attitude of combatively butting. Note that the symbolism of the lamb is by no means the same. It pertains rather to Tiphereth in the formula of the Æon of Osiris. This is all probably derived from the fact that lamb is the tenderest meat obtainable and therefore the priests insisted on lamb being sacrificed for their benefit. The true nature of the Lamb would be rather Venusian or Lunar, but it would be better to cut it altogether out of the symbolic scheme, because of the priestly connection which the idea has suffered. The Owl is sacred to Aries as the bird of Minerva.

16. The Bull is the Kerub of Earth. All beasts of burden and those used in agriculture may be attributed here.

17. All animals of dual nature in any respect pertain partly to Gemini. The Magpie is especially sacred to this sign because of its piebald plumage and its power of speech. The Parrot is given here for similar reasons. The Zebra is here on account of its stripes. All hybrids pertain to Gemini, both on account of their dual nature and because they are sterile like Mercury. The Penguin is here as superficially imitating man.

18. The Crab pertains to Cancer as the translation of the word. The Turtle is found among the symbols of the Court Cards of the suit of Cups. The Whale suggests Cancer because of its power of blowing water, and its faculty, in incorrect tradition, of swallowing large objects such as prophets. All beasts of transport may be attributed here in reference to ATU VII.

19. Leo means Lion and is the Kerub of Fire. The Cat is of the Lion family, so also is the Tiger. The Serpent is given to Leo because the letter Teth means Serpent. There is an important mystery concealed in ATU XI, and Woman may be attributed to Leo in respect to her sexual ferocity through which she dominates Man; that is, the lower element in Man, especially his courage as represented by the Lion.

20. All animals which go solitary are attributed here, as also those which refuse to unite with others. This is connected not only with ATU IX but with the cold-bloodedness of Mercury. The Rhinoceros—the single horn suggests Mercury, line 8. In the Dhammapada he is taken as the emblem of the Hermit.

22. The Elephant is given to Libra because equilibrium is the basis of the Universe. The symmetry of any animal is of the nature of Libra, and so we may place in this group any animals which make symmetrical patterns; as, for instance, the Spider (see line 6). But even the Spiders which live in the earth build their houses with a great regularity.

24. Scorpio means Scorpion. The Beetle is given to Scorpio chiefly on account of the peculiar colour (see the Empress Scale, Column XVIII) and partly because of certain habits, such as its transmutation through putrefaction. All reptiles may be placed here for this reason.

The Lobster and Crayfish are, so to speak, water scorpions. The Shark is one of the most martial inhabitants of the sea. The Crablouse refers to Scorpio both by nature and habitat.

25. The Centaur is traditionally connected with Archery, besides being partly a horse; the horse itself is connected with the idea of hunting and speed. Note that the speed of Sagittarius, which is the flickering of a dying fire, is not to be confused with the speed of Mercury, which is the speed of thought or electricity. The Hippogriff combines the Horse of Mars with the Eagle of Jupiter. The Dog is sacred to the huntress Artemis.

26. Capricornus means Goat. The Ass and the Oyster are traditionally sacred to Priapus. An animal is sacred to Capricorn in respect of its ambition, actual or symbolic. It is the leaping of the Goat and its fondness for high and barren mountains which connect it with Capricorn, the sign which represents the zenith in the Zodiac. Note that the sexual instinct should primarily be regarded as indicative of the ambition or aspiration of the animal to higher things.

28. See line 11 for the first attribution. The Peacock is the bird of Juno as Lady of Air and especially Aquarius, but the Peacock might also be referred to Tiphereth or even to Mercury and Sagittarius on account of its plumage. The vision of the Universal Peacock is connected with the Beatific Vision, in which the Universe is perceived as a whole in every part, as the essence of joy and beauty; but in its diversity this is connected with the symbolism of the Rainbow, which refers to the middle stage in Alchemical working, when the Matter of the Work takes on a diversity of flashing colours. This, however, is connected not so much with the nature of Sagittarius in itself as an isolated constellation, but with its position on the Tree of Life as leading from Yesod to Tiphereth. Samekh must therefore be regarded in this matter as the threshold of Tiphereth, even as Gimel is the threshold of Kether, and Tau of Yesod. These three, therefore, constitute the three main balanced spiritual experiences in the way of attainment.

29. Pisces means Fish, but, as previously indicated, actual fish do

not belong here so much as to Mercury. The Dolphin pertains to Pisces, principally because Venus is exalted in the sign, while its ruler, Jupiter, is also implied in that attribution of which we see the outcome in the title of the Heir-apparent to the Crown of France. The Beetle is Kephra, the Sun at mightnight, who is shown travelling through the Pool of Night in ATU XVIII. Pisces, moreover, is that greatest darkness before the dawn of the year in the parallel symbolism. There is also a mystery in the fact that the Beetle rolls up of ball of dung, thus constructing the Sun from the excrement of putrefaction. As it is written, "It is from the excrement of Choronzon that one takes the material for the creation of a God."* The Jackal is shown in ATU XVIII. He also feeds on excrement. The sign Pisces represents the apparent stagnation of the Work, its final decomposition. And it is at this moment that it is brought by the Redeemer—who has descended into the lowest hell for the purpose—across the threshold into the higher sphere. Note that it is because of the condition of the experiment that the Work necessarily lends itself to every form of glamour and illusion. Its nature is certain to be misinterpreted even by the Redeemer himself, insofar as he is compelled to fix his attention upon the Matter of the Work and so to lose sight for the moment of the essential Truth which underlies its appearances. The Dog is attributed to Pisces on account of his being sacred to the Moon, the title of ATU XVIII. The Dogs baying at the Moon, with the accompanying assumption of witchcraft and all that type of phenomena which we associate with the treacherous semi-darkness of the waning moon, are shown in some versions of the Trumps by artists who did not understand the deeper symbolism of Kephra and Anubis. That false representation is exactly characteristic of the sort of thing that always is to be expected to occur in connection with the work of the Magician in this sign.

---

* [Misquoted from *Book 4* Part II, cap. 6 (p. 62 in first edition), which had "It is from the rubbish-heap of Choronzon that one selects the material for a god!"

COLUMN XXXIX: THE PLANTS

o. The Lotus and Rose are attributed to 0 because they have traditionally been taken as glyphs of the circle.

1. The Amond in flower is connected with Aaron's Rod that budded. The Almond is the proper wood for the wand of the White magician, but the attribution should really be to the middle pillar as a whole. The branches of the Banyan tree take fresh roots where they touch the ground and start new main stems: this is connected with the special idea of Kether implied in the Philosophy given in the Commentary on the *Book of the Law*.

2. The Amaranth is the flower of immortality. It is here placed in order to symbolize that quality of the Yod of Tetragrammaton, the principle of Chiah. The Mistletoe is given for a similar reason. The Bo or Pipal tree was the shelter of Buddha at the moment of his enlightenment. Furthermore, its leaves suggest the phallus.

3. The Cypress pertains to Saturn. The Opium Poppy is connected with sleep, night and understandings. The Lotus is the general feminine symbol. The Lily suggests the purity of the Great Mother. The Ivy has dark leaves and its clinging nature reminds us of feminine or curving growth.

4. The Olive is attributed to Jupiter because of its softness and richness. Its colour furthermore suggests that of the watery part of Malkuth in the Queen Scale (Column XVI). The Shamrock of four leaves, a good-luck plant, suggests Jupiter. The Opium Poppy is Jupiterian as giving relief from pain, quiet, and olympian detatchment.

5. The Oak and Hickory are attributed here because of the hardness of their wood. Nux Vomica, on account of its tonic properties and the action of strychnine in causing the contraction of muscles with convulsive violence. The Nettle, on account of its burning sting.

6. The Oak is also, and more properly, attributed to Tiphereth because it was the sacred tree of the Druids, the representative in the vegetable kingdom of the Sun. Its strength is also taken as harmonious with that quality in man. Furthermore, the Acorn is peculiarly phallic,

and this is properly to be attributed to Tiphereth because in this case the phallic symbol contains in itself the essence of the being to be reproduced. The Acacia is placed here as a symbol of resurrection as in the rituals of Free Masonry. The Bay and Laurel are sacred to Apollo, the Vine to Dionysus. Gorse, the sacred flower of the A∴A∴ was chosen as their heraldic emblem to be a symbol of the Great Work. Its appearance is that of the Sun in full blaze, and suggests the burning bush of Moses. Its branches are exceedingly firm, as should be the Will of the Adept, and they are covered with sharp spikes, which symbolize, on the one hand, the phallic energy of the Will and, on the other, the pains which are glady endured by one who puts forth his hand to pluck this bloom of sunlight splendour. Note that the Great Work is here concentrated in Tiphereth, the attainment of the Grade corresponding to which is in fact the critical stage on the Path of the Wise. The Ash is one of the most important of the solar trees; the wood is firm and elastic. The World-Ash represents the microcosm in legend. Yggdrasil is itself an Ash. Aswata, the World-Fig, should also be attributed here as the Tree itself in the microcosm.

7. The Rose has always been a special flower of Venus. The Laurel is included because a wreath of these leaves is a symbol of victory.

8. Moly is mentioned in Homer as having been given by Hermes to Ulysses to counteract the spells of Circe. It has a black root and white blossom, which again suggests the dual currents of energy. *Anhalonium Lewinii** has for one of its principal characteristics the power to produce very varied and brilliant colour visions.

9. The Banyan is given here for the same reason as that in line 1. It is, so to speak, the foundation of a system of trees as Yesod is the foundation of the branches of the Tree of Life. The Mandrake is the typically phallic plant. It is peculiarly adapted to use in sexual magic, and it does have a direct connection with the automatic consciousness which has its seat in Yesod. Damiana is reputed a powerful aphrodisiac, and so are Ginseng and Yohimba.

---

* [Now *Lophophora williamsi*; the peyote cactus.]

10. The Willow is the traditional tree of the neglected maiden, Malkuth unredeemed. The Lily suggests that maiden's purity, and the Ivy her clinging and flexible nature. All Cereals pertain to Malkuth, Wheat being the foundation of the Pentacle which represents Nephesch. The Pomegranate is sacred to Proserpine; in appearance also it is strongly suggestive of the feminine symbol.

THE ELEMENTS

11. Aspen resembles Air, by its trembling.

23. The Lotus is the traditional planet of Water. Its roots are in water and its purity further suggests the action of water in lustration.

31. The Red Poppy is given in this place only on account of its colour, and the same is true of Hibiscus. All scarlet flowers might be equally well placed here. But the attribution is not very satisfactory, as the nature of flowers in themselves is not usually fiery except as their perfume is a stimulant.

32 bis. The Oak is given on account of its stability, and the Ivy because of the analogy of Earth with Malkuth. All Cereals pertain here, Wheat, the typical cereal, being the foundation of the Pentacle.

31 bis. For Almond see line 1. It should be generally remarked with regard to the elemental attributions in this column that the seed should be taken as representing Spirit with a slight admixture of Fire, the stem as Fire, the blossom as Water, the leaf as Air, and the fruit as Earth. Note that the fruit usually contains the seed of the new generation exactly as the Empresses are called the Thrones of Spirit.

THE PLANETS

12. The attributions given here are traditional. The Palm is Mercurial, as being hermaphrodite. The Lime or Linden tree is Mercurial because of its pale yellow fruit with a peculiarly clean-tasting pulp.

13. These attributions are again traditional. The Hazel is suitable for the wand of the Black magician whose typical deity is the Moon just as that of the White magician is the Sun. The Pomegranate is also attributed here as a symbol with reference to menstruation. The Alder has a soft spongy wood which gives very little heat when burned. It haunts

watery spots.

14. These are traditional also. The Fig is Venusian on account of its sexual symbolism. The Peach belongs to Venus on account of its soft beauty and sweetness, the external splendour of its bloom being easily brushed off, its tendency to rot and the prussic acid in its kernel. The Apple is traditionally appropriate to Venus on account of the legend of the Fall. There are however various traditions concerning the Tree of Knowledge of Good and Evil.

21. The Hyssop is Jupiterian on account of its religious use in lustration. It might perhaps be more properly attributed to Chesed. The Oak is traditionally sacred to Jupiter, perhaps because it is the king of the trees as Jupiter is king of the gods. The Poplar is given on account of its soft and easily swollen wood and because of its great height. The Fig is Jupiterian because of its soft, swollen and, so to speak, sensual pulp; and also perhaps because of its rich purple colour, suggesting episcopal vestments. Arnica is attributed to Jupiter for its use in relieving pain. Cedar has a traditional value in religious work—its perfume is devotional according to the testimony of intuition, and it is supposed to preserve things in its neighbourhood from the attacks of moths, etc.

27. Absinthe and Rue—these attributions are traditional.

30. The first three attributions are obvious. The Nut is solar, as being a microcosm of Life, the fruit being also the seed. Galangan is specially sacred to the Sun; it is of the ginger family.

32. The Ash is given in connection with the phrase "ashen pale." (The real nature of the tree is more properly solar.) In the other cases, in connection with the ideas of death, melancholy, poison, etc. The Elm is Saturnian on account of its murderous habit of dropping boughs without warning. The wood is also traditionally the best available the best available for coffins.

THE ZODIAC

15. The Olive is sacred to Minerva, but Geranium has a scarlet variety which is precisely the colour of Aries in the King Scale. The

Tiger Lily is a traditional attribution.

16. Again traditional. We might possibly add giant trees of all species to this sign.

17. Hybrids are here for the same reason as in the previous column. Orchids might perhaps better be attributed to Yesod or Capricorn for obvious reasons; they are found here on account of their duplex characteristics.

18. The Lotus is the typical flower of Water and the Moon.

19.*

20. The Snowdrop and the Lily suggest the modest purity of the sign. Narcissus refers to the solitary tradition. Mistletoe is indicated by the macroscopic appearance of semen.

22. This attribution is traditional.

24. The Cactus has watery pulp poisonous spikes. The Nettle is treacherously Martial. All treacherous and poisonous planets may be attributed to Scorpio.

25. The Rush is used for making arrows.

26. Yohimba—see line 9. Thistle is hard, stubborn and spikely. Orchis root is connected with the Cult of Pan. Indian Hemp is tough and fibrous, thus used for making ropes; but see the Column XLIII dealing with vegetable drugs for other properties of this plant.

28. Cocoanut; this attribution is doubtful. There may be some connection with Juno as giving milk or with the symbol of the Waterbearer, because the tree gives us fruit from the air.

29. Opium is given because of its power to produce a peaceful dreamy condition which is liable to end in a stagnation of the mental faculties. Unicellular Organisms are possibly attributed here because they are so frequently found in pool. The Mangrove is not merely a tree of the swamp, but actually produces swamps.

---

* [No explanation given, not that one was needed. — T.S.]

COLUMN XL: PRECIOUS STONES

0. These attributions are somewhat bold. The Star Sapphire refers to Nuit and the Black Diamond to the idea of NOX—Zero. It is invisible yet contains light and structure in itself.

1. The Diamond is white brilliance; it is pure carbon, the foundation of all living structure. The atomic weight is 12, the number of Hua, the title of Kether (but this is a reference to the Zodiac which makes the connection with Zero, on the one hand, and 2, on the other).

2. The Star Ruby represents the male energy of the Creator Star. Turquoise suggests Mazloth, so also does the Star Sapphire, but this would be the sphere of Chokmah not its positive attribution.

3. The Star Sapphire suggests the expanse of night with the Star appearing in the midst thereof. Note that this light is not in the stone itself but is due to the internal structure. The doctrine is that the stars are formed in the body nof night by virtue of the form of the night by the impact fo the energy of a higher plane. The Pearl is referred to Binal on account of its being the typical stone of the sea. It is formed by concentric spheres of hard brilliant substance, the centre being a particle of dust. Thus, that dust which is all that remains of the Exempt Adept after he has crossed the Abyss, is gradually surrounded by sphere after sphere of shining splendour, so that he vbecomes a fitting ornament for the bosom of the Great Mother.

4. Lapiz Lazuli is of the blue violet of the highest form of Jupiter. The specks in it may perhaps be taken to represent those particles of dust referred to above. The Amethyst is the violet of Jupiter. It is the traditional stone of episcopal rank. Its legendary virtue of protecting its bearer from intoxication indicates its value in lustration. It is the purity of the Exempt Adept which destroys for him the illusion or drunkenness of existence, and therefore enables him to take the great leap into the Abyss. The Sapphire pertains to Chesed because of the blue of water and of Venus (Daleth = 4) in the King Scale (Column XV) and of Jupiter in the Queen Scale (Column XVI).

5. The Ruby represents flaming energy.

6. The Topaz is of the Gold of the Sun. It is also traditionally associated with Tiphereth. The Yellow Diamond suggests the reflection of Kether into Tiphereth.

7. The Emerald is of the green of Venus in the King Scale.

8. The Opal has the varied colours attributed to Mercury.

9. Quartz refers to the foundation. Note that gold is found in Quartz, suggesting the concealed glory of the sexual process.

10. Rock Crystal reminds us of the aphorism: Kether is in Malkuth, and Malkuth in Kether, but after another manner.

THE ELEMENTS

11. Topaz is the pure transparent yellow of Air.

23. The Beryl is the pure transparent blue of Water.

31. The Fire Opal suggests the appearance of fire rising from the blackness of the matter which it consumes.

32 bis. Salt is traditionally sacred to Earth.

31 bis. The Black Diamond has the blackness of the Akasa: it is composed of carbon, the basis of the living elements.

THE PLANETS

12. Opal, see line 8. Agate has the Mercurial yellow, but its hardness indicates a strange Saturnian element in it. It might indeed be attributed to Geburah for its orange tinge and its hardness, but it is not sufficiently pure to rank as a precious stone, and must therefore not be placed among the Sephiroth.

13. The Moonstone is a direct image of the Moon. Pearl and Crystal are given for the suggestion of purity (see lines 3 and 10).

14. Emerald is the colour of Venus in the King Scale (Column XV). Turquiose is the blue of Venus in the Queen Scale (Column XVI), but its tendency is to fade into green. When it does this its value is destroyed, and this reminds us of the external splendour and internal corruption of Nogah.

21. See line 4.

27. See line 5.

30. Chrysolith, as the name implies, is a golden stone.

32. This attribution is traditional: it is the dullness and frequent blackness of Onyx which occasions the reference.

THE ZODIAC

15. Ruby is the scarlet of Aries. It is also one of the hardest of precious stones.

16. Topaz refers to the letter Vau, Tiphereth—see line 6.

17. These stones are given here on account of their polarization of light.

18. Amber is of the colour of Cancer in the King Scale: were it a precious stone, it might be attributed to Chokmah or Binah on account of its electrical properties.

19. The Cat's Eye suggests Leo directly.

20. The Peridot is the colour of Virgo in the King Scale.

22. Emerald is of the colour of Libra in the King Scale.

24. Snakestone suggests Scorpio directly. Greenish Turquoise is attributed here as referring to its putrefaction.

25. Jacinth is Hyacinth, the beautiful boy accidentally killed by Apollo with a quoit, the attribution is therefore somewhat far-fetched—from the blood of the boy to the traditional weapons of his lover.

26. For Black Diamond see line 0 and 32-bis. The reference is to the letter A'ain, the eye. The Black Diamond reminds us of the pupil of the eye, and this eye is the eye of the Most Holy Ancient One; Kether. Capricorn is the zenith of the Zodiac as Kether is of the Sephiroth.

28. Artificial Glass pertains to Aquarius, as being the work of man, the Kerub of Air. Chalcedony suggests the clouds by its appearance.

29. Pearl is referred to Pisces because of its cloudy brilliance as contrasred with the transparency of the other precious stones. It thus reminds us of the astral plane with its semi-opaque visions as opposed to those of pure light which pertain to purely spiritual spheres. One must not emphasize the connection with water; because the Pearl is not found in the type of water characteristic of Pisces.

COLUMN XLI: MAGICAL WEAPONS

The full meaning of these weapons will be found in Book 4, Part II, and in *Magick in Theory and Practice*. Here we can only give brief reasons for their attribution.

0. No magical weapon can be attributed here, for they are all positive. The reduction of the positive to Zero is the goal of all magical work.

1. The Crown is the meaning of Kether. It refers to the Supreme Divinity which the magician assumes in his working. The Swastika symbolize whirling energy, the initiation of all magical force—the Rashith ha-Gilgalim. There is a great deal of varied symbolism in this instrument, notably sexual; it demands a great deal of study to appreciate fully the virtue of this weapon. The Lamp is not a weapon; it is a light shining from above which illuminates the whole work.

2. The Lingam is the symbol of the Chiah, the creative energy. The Inner Robe symbolizes the true self of the magician, his "unconscious" as the psychoanalysts call it. Their description, however, of its characteristic is totally incorrect. The Word is the intellegible expression of the Will of the creative energy of the Magus.

3. The Yoni represents Neschamah. The Outer Robe refers to the darkness of Binah. The A∴A∴ star refers to the aspiration. The Cup receives the influence from the Highest. It must be distinguished emphatically from the wand or hollow tube of Chokmah which transmits the influence in its positive form in an intelligible manner but without understanding its nature.

4. The Wand is the reflection of the Lingam as the paternal power of Chesed in the solidification of the male creative energy of Chokmah. The Sceptre is the weapon of authority referrring to Jupiter (Gedulah—magnificence). The Crook is the weapon of Chesed—Mercy as opposed to the scourge of Geburah.

5. The Scourge is the weapon of severity as opposed to the Crook. This is the explanation of those two weapons being crossed in the hands of the risen Osiris. The Sword is the weapon of Mars, so also is the

Spear. These weapons emphasize the fiery energy in the creative Lingam. The Chain represents the severity of the restrictions which must be placed on wandering thoughts: it might more properly be attributed to Daath. It does not really exist on the magician himself. Its function is to bind that which is above all Not-He. It is thus the only weapon which does not possess a definite unity of form and which has multiple units in its composition.

6. The Lamen represents the symbolic form of the Human Will and Consciousness of the magician. The Rosy Cross is technically pertinent to Tiphereth.

7. The Lamp carried in the hand pertains to Netzach because Love must be enkindled by the magician. It throws light as required on particular objects. This Lamp must in no wise be confused with that of Kether. The Girdle is the traditional weapon of Venus. It represents the ornament of beauty. When it is untied it can be used to bind and blind-fold the candidate. It thus represents the power of fascination by love.

8. The Names and Versicles are Mercurial. They expand the Logos, explain it in three-dimensional (that is, material) terms, just as the number 8 is a three-dimensional expansion of the number 2. The Apron conceals the Splendour (Hod) of the magician. It also explains that splendour by virtue of its symbolic design.

9. The Perfumes pertain to Yesod as forming a link between earth and heaven. This link is material by virtue of the substance of the incense, and spiritual by virtue of thie action through the olfactory sense upon the consciousness. The Sandals enable the magician to "travel on the firmament of Nu." The Sandal-strap is the Ankh which represents the mode of going, going being the essential faculty of every god. This strap, whose form is that of the Rosy Cross, forms a link between the material apparatus of his going and his feet; that is to say, the formula of the Rosy Cross enables a man to go—or, in other words, endows him with Godhead. The Altar is the foundation of the operation. Its characteristic is stability; also it resembles Yesod as supporting the Ruach; that is to say, the means of the Formative World (Ruach = Yetzirah) through which it is proposed to work. The Altar and the

sacrifice might also as well have been attributed to Tiphereth. This would, in fact, be actually better in the case of certain types of operation, such as invocations of the Holy Guardian Angel, for in this case the human heart is the foundation of the work.

10. The Circle and Triangle are the spheres of operation of the magician and his work which is in Malkuth, the kingdom, the Realm of Assiah. The Triangle being outside the Circle, is the place of the Spirit, but it belongs not to him for his realm is formlessness. The Triangle is the figure into which Choronzon must be evoked in order to confer form upon him.

THE ELEMENTS

11. The Dagger, the characteristic elemental weapon of Air. The Fan—this symbolzes the power to direct the forces of Air.

23. The Cross of Suffering refers to the now superseded formula of Osiris. See the original emblem of the Hermetic Order of the Golden Dawn, a triangle surmounted by a Cross. The Cup is the traditional elemental weapon of Water. The Wine fills the Cup—it is the divine ecstasy entering the receptive part of the nature of the magician. The Water of Lustration in the Cup of the Stolistes balances the Fire in the thurible of the Dadouchos.

31. The Wand is the elemental weapon of Fire. It is not to be confused with the Wand of Chokmah or Chesed any more than the Cup of Water is to be mistaken for that of Binah. The Elemental weapons are but vice-regents of the true weapons of the Sephiroth. The thurible or lamp is borne by the Dadouchos to consecrate the candidate with fire. The Pyramid of Fire is an altogether minor weapon and is only used in certain ceremonies of uncommon type.*

32 bis. The Pantacle is the elemental weapon of Earth. The platter of bread and salt, or sometimes salt alone, is its equivalent, but is used actively to administer to the candidate sometimes to seal his obligation, sometimes to nourish him spiritually. Bread and Salt are the two principal substances traditionally sacred to Earth.

* [The reference is possibly to one of the Golden Dawn admission badges. — T.S.]

31 bis. The Winged Egg is symbolical of the spiritualized phallic energy. The Egg is Akasa, the source of all creation. There are many equivalent symbols.

THE PLANETS

12. The Wand is that of the Will or Word, the Logos. The Caduceus is the legendary wand of Mercury, and to be carefully distinguished from the hollow tube of Chokmah. It represents the Middle Pillar crowned by the Winged Globe of Kether. It is thus the plumed phallus as distinguished from the Phoenix-crowned phallus of animal-life creation through the initiaiton of Fire (see line 19), and the flowering phallus of the Lotus-crowned Wand of Isis, the wand of vegetable-life creation through the initiation of Water (see line 20). The Serpents of the Caduceus, the positive and negative forms of energy, resume the powers of these two wands.

13. The Bow and Arrow are traditionally the weapons of Artemis and Apollo (see line 30).

14. See line 7.

21. See line 4. The Sceptre is not a true weapon. It is the symbol of authority, an ornamental reminder of the wand which is kept in the background. The Sceptre must not be used to strike, it would break: as soon as its virtue is challenged, it must be instantly discarded for the thunderbolt.

27. This Sword is not to be confused with the Dagger of Air. It represents the active and militant energy of the magician. Its true form is the flaming sword, the lightning flash, which strikes down from Kether through the Sephiroth as a zig-zag flash. It destroyed by dividing the unity of that against which its energies are directly. It is ultimately an error to identify the sword with the wand as a phallic symbol though this is often done. In the Lesser Mysteries of "John" the sword and disk repressent the Wand and cup of the Greater Mysteries of "Jesus." In the former, John the Baptist's head is removed by sword (air) and presented on a charger, the platter or disk of earth. In the latter, the heart of Jesus is pierced by the Spear, the Wand of Fire, and

the blood collected in the Cup or Graal (water). But the Sword and Disk are not sufficiently sacred to be truly phallic. This is one of the subtle distinctions which afford the key to the finest spiritual comprehension.

30. The Lamen is solar, as representing the light of the human consciousness—in the Heart (Tiphereth)—of the magician to the spirit evoked. It is his statement to the spirit of his intention towards it, of the formula which he intends to employ; it must in no wise be confused with the Pantacle, which is passive as the Lamen is active. The one represeents the condition of things in general, the other his method of dealing with that condition. Bow and Arrow—see line 13.

32. The Sickle is the traditional weapon of Saturn. It implies the power of time to reap the harvest of man's life and work. It may be used in actual ceremony to threaten the spirit that Choronzon will cut short his independent existence, that Choronzon will reap his Karma, and add it to the treasure of Choronzon's storehouse.

THE ZODIAC

15. The Horns are those of the Ram; they signify the power of thought, the energy of Minerva. The Burin is used for engraving the Lamen, Pantacles, etc. Being a Knife, its character is martial, but also it pertains especially to Aries because it is used to indicate the creative ideas of the magician.

16. The Throne refers to Vau: the Heart must support and admit the lordship of the higher consciousness of the magician. The Altar may also be attributed to Taurus on account of its solidity and its function of bearing the higher elements of the magician. There is a mystery of Europa and Pasiphaë connected with this attribution.

17. The Tripod would appear at first sight to be Lunar; but this is wrong. The real connection is with ATU VI, the "Oracle of the Mighty Gods."

18. The Furnace is connected with the eargy of the Sun in Cancer. The Cup is the Holy Graal.

19. The Phoenix Wand—see line 12.

20. The Lamp and Wand appear in ATU IX as the weapons of the Hermit. This Wand is concealed: it is the virile energy reserved. This

Lamp has the same significance and is not to be confused with other lamps. The Bread is the natural product, the fertile earth; it convey sacramentally, "every word that cometh out of the mouth of God." The Lotus Wand—see line 12.

22. The Cross of Equilibrium is impled or expressed in every part of the arrangements of the Temple. The Balances, or Witnesses, as shown in ATU VIII, are in actual practice concealed with the Sword. They represent the complete phallus, the secret weapon, which alone can satisfy; that is, do justice to Nature.

24. The Oath is the formula of transmutation. The Serpent is connected with several of the magical weapons, and implies the secret kingly power of the magician, the essense of the phallic energy as employed in transmutation.

25. The Arrow is sacred to the rainbow symbolism. It represents especially the spritualization of the magical energy, being a missle sped through the air, no longer connected physically with the material form of the magician.

26. Compare line 20.

28. The Censer carries the perfumes as the clouds carry the distillation of the water of earth. The Aspergillus similarly sprinkles the lustral waters as the clouds shed rain.

29. Magical operations are usually performed in an artificial twilight; this represents the glamour of the astral plane which the magician proposes to illume with the divine light. The natural attribution of this idea is evidently ATU XVIII. The Magic Mirror reflects astral forms. It is evidently cognate with the still waters of Pisces, and the entire symbolism is again obviously that of ATU XVIII.

COLUMN XLII: PERFUMES

These attributions are founded for the most part upon tradition. Some of them are connected with legend, others are derived from clairvoyant observation. The rational basis of attribution is, therefore, less apparent in this column than in those of the Gods, Magical Weapons, etc.

0. No attribution can be made here, 0 being the goal of a magical operation by love under will, and any perfume will be an expression of that love under will itself.

1. Ambergris has comparatively little perfume of its own, but it has a virtue of bringing out the best of any others with which it may be mixed. In the same way, Kether cannot be said to have any intrinsic qualities, but its influence brings out the highest faculties of those ideas which it illuminates.

2. The orchitic origin of Musk indicates Chokmah. This is the male aspect of the Work.

3. Civet, "the uncleanly flux of a cat," corresponds to Musk as Binah to Chokmah, its origin being feminine. Myrrh is traditionally the odour of sorrow and bitterness; it is the dark and passive side of Binah.

"Brothers, I have brought him myrrh.
Sorrow black and sinister
Shall his name bring to the race."*

"My incense is of resinous woods and gums; and there is no blood therein: because of my hair the trees of Eternity."†

4. See Column XXXIX.

5. Tobacco. This attribution is due to Frater D.D.S. (who was a chemist). It seems to me not altogether satisfacory. The idea is presumably that it is the favourite perfume for men engaged in hard work.

6. The correctness of this should be intuitively perceived at once by every magician. Olibanum possesses a comprehensive catholic quality such as no other incense can boast.

7. The sensuous seductiveness of Benzoin is unmistakable. Contrast with line 24. Rose naturally suggests the more physical aspects of the feminine symbol. Civet, however, is much more strongly sexual than Rose, but this implies a more intense element of spirituality. The student must eliminate completely from his mind any idea that sex is

---

* [Crowley, *The World's Tragedy*, Act III. The New Falcon printing has "Mother, I have brought ..." I do not know which reading is correct. — T.S.]
† [*AL* I. 59.]

naturally gross. On the contrary, even the lowest manifestations of it in its pure form are less material than such ideas as are represented by Rose. Demonic, not material, developments follow the degradation of the instinct. Red Sandal is Venusian, intuitively by its smell, and sensibly by its colour. The attribution is further guaranteed by the usefulness of its oil as a specific of gonorrhoea.

    8. Storax is chiefly Mercurial on account of its nondescript nature. It is really less valuable as a perfume itself than as a menstruum for other perfumes, in the same was as Mercury is the basis of amalgams. But Storax is really to dark and heavy to bew a really adequate perfume for Hod.

    9. Jasmin is traditionally sacred, especially in Persia, to the spiritual use of the generative process. Ginseng—see Column XXXIX. Roots are sacred to Yesod as the reproductive function is the root of the life of man. It is important not to suppose that Malkuth, Nephesch, is the root of reality. Malkuth is a pendant to the Tree, a sensory illusion which enables it to perceive itself.

    10. Dittany of Crete was said by Blavatsky to be the most powerful of all magical perfumes. This is true in a limited sense. Its smoke is the best basis for material magical manifestations of all those menstrua which are not animal. It is quite as catholic as Olibanum in character but has no positive element in its composition. Further, its velvet softness and its silvery bloom remind one of Betulah. There are many allusions in classical traditions to Dittany, which all point to the same attribution.

THE ELEMENTS

    11. Galbanum represents the element of Air in that exceedingly powerful incense of Tetragrammaton whose invention is ascribed to Moses.

    23. Onycha represents Water in the incense of Moses. It is now very difficult to obtain, though at one time I possessed a supply. Its origin is somehow connected with certain shellfish. Myrrh—see line 3.

    31. Olibanum is the fiery elemental incense of Moses.

32 bis. Storax is the earth elemental incense of Moses.
31 bis. No attribution can be made here. See line 1.

THE PLANETS

At one time or another mediæval writers on magic have attributed every possible incense to every possible planet. Tradition, therefore, gives little to us in this investigation, while the sense of smell varies enormously. One may almost say it is impossible for any two people to agree about any given perfume, and when they occur in combination, the diversity of opinion is even more striking. The spiritual bearing of the perception is naturally yet more illusive and indeterminate. The attributions given in this column may be considered perfectly reliable, being based as far as possible upon considerations of essential virtue, independent of sensation. Nevertheless, it is incumbent upon the student to undertake experimental investigations in every case. A proper comprehension of the virtues of perfumes is of the utmost importance to the work of the Adeptus Major, for they constitute the most vital link between the material and astral planes, and it is precisely this link which the Adeptus Major most intimately needs.

The method of burning the perfumes is of much greater importance than is generally understood. Except for material workings, the gross body of the incense should not be carbonized. The heat applied should be only that sufficient to drive off the essential aromatic substance. In many cases it is best to evaporate the essential oil previously extracted secundum artem.

The thurible should be of the (properly consecrated) metal appropriate to the incense; mixed perfumes should be burned on silver or gold, preferably gold. Failure to obtain the utmost possible perfection in any of these points is often sufficient to vitiate the most elaborate ceremony.

12. Mastic is pale yellow, and its perfume is singularly clean and free from any prejudice (to use a somewhat strange term) either for or against any particular moral idea. Its action on other perfumes is usually to intensify them and quicken their rate of vibration. White

Sandal is free from the sensuousness of its Red twin. Note that the sympathy of Mercury and Venus is very strong, but it resembles that of the epicene adolescent, the Amazon maiden on the languishing boy, as opposed to the definitely sexualized youth in the romantic period of rose-coloured spectacles. Nutmeg is probably attributed to Mercury on account of its yellowish tinge. White Mace, the husk which covers it, is Mercurial. Red Mace is probably solar. Storax—see line 8. Fugitive odours are Mercurial for the obvious reasons.

13. The attribution of Menstrual Fluid to Luna depends not only on the periodicity, but on the fact that Luna is herself the symbolical vehicle of the solar light. Camphor—the white waxen appearance suggests Luna, so also the perfume is peculiarly cleanly. It is supposed by some to be useful as a disinfectant. It is in fact useful against moths. This is sympathetic with the idea of lustration. The Mexican Aloes furnishes an alcoholic drink, Pulque, whose cloudy whiteness suggests Luna. Lignum Aloes is a wood in powder, whose physical appearance suggests purity of aspiration to the sensitive observer. The connection is therefore directly with the Path of Gimel—see line 25. Virginal odours obviously suggest the Virgin Moon. Sweet odours are also lunar, because the moon represents the physical senses and refers to the common people. Similarly sugar and sweet things generally are much liked by children (who are classed under Luna) and by that vast herd of mankind, and espcially those woman whose sense of taste is not sufficiently refined to appreciate real delicateness. Sweetness masks all finer qualities unless they be peculiarly violent: hence the use of sugar, chloroform water and similar compounds to conceal the unpleasant taste of certain medicines.

14. Sandalwood—see line 7. Myrtle, the traditional plant of Venus. Softness and voluptuousness are two of the principle qualities of Venus.

21. Saffron has brilliant purple filaments. An orange dye is prepared from it which indicates the solar nature. But this is sympathetic to Jupiter, and in any case refers to a watery element in its nature, whereas this column deals with the airy constituents of the substance described. The perfume of Saffron is intuitively perceived as generous,

rich, and suggesting the sensuous enjoyment of devotion.

27. Pepper is evidently Martial owing to its fiery qualitiy and its specific action on the mucous membrane of the nostrils. Dragon's Blood gives off a dark red smoke, is angry looking, unpleasant to smell, and intuitively perceived as smouldering irritability. Heat and pungency are two principle qualities of Mars.

30. Olibanum—see line 6, Cinnamon—the appearance is decidedly solar; any martial element therein is not confirmed by the perfume, which resembles that of a hot summer day, in the opinion of many sensitives. It is also solar on account of its cordial and carminative properties. "Glorious" is the prime epithet of the external character of Sol. By "glorious odours" are meant those which arouse in the percipient sensations of enjoyment of well-being, with possibly the influx of a certain quality of pride.

32. There is little difficultly in recognizing Saturnian perfumes; the difficulty in practice is to find one which is at all tolerable to the sense of smell. In magical work of the kind which borders upon the material plane, large quantities of incense are necessary and incantation becomes difficult when the magician is being rapidly asphyxiated. The Adeptus Major can indeed cut himself off from such inconveniences but it is otherwise for the beginner. This is one more of the many reasons which have caused teachers to warn their pupils against attempting to work on the plane of Saturn until they are far advanced. Yet this caution exposes the dsiciple to an even worse danger than that of being choked, which is to formulate an incomplete and unbalanced universe. Assafoetida—pure samples are not intolerably unpleasant. Scammony is repulsive, principally because of its suggestion of domestic cookery. Indigo furnishes a smoke of the characteristic dark blue of Saturn; the smoke is composed of very solid particles; and this perfume is accordingly both wholly in keeping with the nature of the Planet and pre-eminently suitable for material workings. Sulphur. This is the most difficult incense with which to work. It is liable to provoke fits of coughing, and may even be dangerous, but it is certainly the most usesful in conjuration of the infernal powers. (By "Evil" is meant

principally that quality which threates the magician with failure and, philosophically speaking, this qualitiy is pre-eminently the category of Time, which is Saturn.)

THE ZODIAC

15. See line 27.

16. It may be doubted whether the indifference of Storax, referred to in line 8, is really Mercurial: it might almost equally well be the neutrality of dullness, the characteristic of the passive laborious earth. The perfume of Storax suggests the patience of cattle, and even physical the peculiar sweetish scent of a cowshed.

17. Wormwood probably pertains to Gemini on account of the intellectual stimulation which it affords in such a magical preparation as Absinthe.

18. See line 23.

19. Olibanum, combining the ideas of fire and Sol, is pre-eminently suited to Leo, the Kerub of Fire, the house of the Sun.

20. See Column XXXIX.

22. See line 11. Galbanum has a peculiar scent which intuitively suggests danger or even evil. There is a hint of hidden treachery, which is nevertheless seductive. This refers to the exaltation of Saturn in Libra, the house of Venus, which refers to the impregnation of the idea of Love by that of Death. It recalls the rape of Persephone by Hades; or, more appropriately still, that tragic element in love which has formed a theme of all great poets, from Aeschylus and Homer to Shakespeare and Goethe.

24. Siamese Benzoin is to be distinguished from that found in other countries. It has a peculiar odour strongly suggestive of the treachery of the snake. It is the hidden poison not unlike that of Galbanum. The voluptuousness of the perfume is of that type of debauchery whose fascination is directly connected with the knowledge of its fatal issue. Opoponax refers even more directly to Scorpio than does Siamese Benzoin. There is in it even less of the sensuousness of pleasure; there is an overpowering richness of the deliciously abominable.

25. See line 13. The perfume of Lignum Aloes intuitively suggests horsemanship in an airy racecourse, as distinguished from charioteering, as if one's racecourse were a rainbow. One experiences the intense amazon purity of Atalanta. One's aspiration becomes winged. It is therefore to Sagittarius, not as the house of Jupiter, but as the path leading from Yesod to Tiphereth, that this perfume applies.

26. Musk and Civet are referred here on account of their sexual origin, and of their effect upon the aura of the magician. The regular Saturnian perfumes would only be employed in amefic work and in other of the baser aspects of Capricorn.

28. See lines 11 and 22. This attribution is not very satisfactory. There is more in Galbanum than the Saturnian and airy elements. Galbanum is too exciting to be a truly Aquarian perfume; it is too demonic, it lacks the element of humanity. In the humanitarianism of Aquarius there is no magician to understand that "Love is the law, love undew will." It is the smug aloofness of the philanthropist. Certain schools of late years have written very enthusiastically of Aquarius, but their attitude may seem to adherents of the true Rosicrucian doctrine as somewhat hypocritical and pharisaical. This is to be explained by the fact that in Aquarius the Sun is in his detriment. People who wish to reform the world (on a pattern of theoretical excellence totally unconnected with human nature) are at the very antipodes of solar life and light. They fear vitality.

29. See line 13. This Luna of ATU XVIII is to be contrasted strongly with that of ATU II. The path of Gimel leads from Tiphereth to Kether: it is the unswerving virginal aspiration of the human heart to its divine Lord. The postulant at the gate of the Holy of Holies puts off his pride of manhood and offers himself passively as a bride of his sublime Master. His starting point is the perfection of his human self, and his goal the unity of Absolute Truth, above all quantity or quality. On the contrary, the path of Qoph leads from Malkuth to Netzach. It is the fluctuating craving of the animal soul for the sensuous gratifications of illusory victory. By the treacherous light of the waning Moon, the wanderer stumbles through the swamps upon the edge of the black pool

of the Abyss, along the winding path beset by the hell-hounds, up barren slopes to where two "squat turrets, blind as the fool's heart," guard a pass leading he knows not where. His starting point is the illusion of matter, his goal the sphere of external splendour and internal corruption. The path leads away from the middle pillar, to the anarchy of the unbalanced astral wilderness. It is the essence of error. He should rather trust himself to the Bark of the Midnight Sun, the Winged Beetle, to bear him to the Dawn. He should rather follow the path of Tau, passing through the balanced Elements of the astral palne, despite their darkness and their terror. The Menstrual Fluid is, however, the medium for the one as for the other. But on the path of Qoph there is no creative energfy to fertilize the ova, no light to purify and vitalize their possibilities. The path of Qoph is that of witchcraft. The Great Work is not accomplished. The Postulant is not the ecstatic bride who knows that she will be endowed from on high with the great grace of motherhood, but the hag who clutches at the false gratifications of hysteria. Instead of the human consciousness being thrilled directly by the pure light of its One Lord, the animal sensorium is agitated by the confused jabberings of those demons who personate great souls, human or divine. It is the difference between the Knowledge and Conversation of the Holy Guardian Angel and the hideous intimacy with the débris of decaying minds, momenetarily galvanized into manifestation by imbecile of malignant entities.

COLUMN XLIII: VEGETABLE DRUGS

1. Elixir Vitae—the attribution to Kether is due to its omniform virtue.

2. Cocaine pertains to Chokmah by its direct action on the deepest nervous centres.

3. Soma is said to give understanding and was sacred to the highest form of the Moon. Belladonna is here because of its virtue to dilate the pupil, thus producing a Black Sea; but this attribution seems a little fantastic.

4. Opium—its virtue is to relieve pain and to confer philosophic calm.

5. Nux Vomica, Nettle, and Cocaine are given here for their power of excitation in one way or another. The attribution of the last named is doubtful as its apparent stimulating function is really due to its function as a local anæsthetic. Atropine is given here on account of its power to balance the influence of Morphia.

6. These drugs are all direct cardiac stimulants. Alcohol in particular pertains to Bacchus. Further, it is an omniform menstruum for the Astral Light.

7-8. Cannabis Indica and Anhalonium Lewinii appear to act on both these Sephiroth. Their action is very similar. They produce in one mood voluptuous visions which pertain to Venus, and in another confer the power of self-analysis, which is Mercurial.

9. This attribution refers to its alleged aphrodisiac action.

10. Corn is the typical stimulant of the Nephesch as such.

COLUMN XLV: MAGICAL POWERS

The attributions in this column explain themselves: they are direct representations in spiritual or magical experience of the natures of the various components of the Key Scale.

Add: 0. Vision of No Difference.

         2. Vision of Antinomies.

         3. Vision of Wonder.

         6. Beatific Vision.

        25. Vision of Universal Peacock.

        32. Travels on the Astral Plane.

COLUMNS LVI-LXVIII, LXXVII-LXXXVI, XCVII

These attributions are all traditional.

ON THE NATURE AND SIGNIFICANCE
OF THE MAGICAL ALPHABET

The book 777 has for its primary object the construction of a magical alphabet.

One of the greatest difficulties experienced by the student—a difficulty which increases rather than diminishes with his advance in knowledge"is this: he finds it impossible to gain any clear idea of the meanings of the terms which he employs. Every philosopher has his own meaning, even for such universally used terms as soul; and in most cases he does not so much as suspect that other writers use the term under a different connotation. Even technical writers and those who take the trouble to define their terms before using them are too often at variance with each other. The diversity is very great in the case of this word soul. It is sometimes used to mean Atman, an impersonal principle almost synonymous with the Absolute—itself a word which has been defined with scores of different senses. Others use it to mean the personal individual soul as distinguished from the over-soul or God. Others take it as equivalent to Neschamah, the Understanding, the intelligible essence of man, his aspiration; yet others mean the Nephesch, the animal soul, the consciousness corresponding to the senses. It has even been identified with the Ruach which is really the mechanism of the mind. Apart from these major distinctions there are literally hundreds of minor shades of meanings. We find therefore a writer predicating the soul A, B, and C, while his fellow student protests vehemently that it is none of these things—despinte which the two men may be in substantial agreement.

Let us suppose for a moment that by some miracle we obtain a clear idea of the meaning of the word. The trouble has merely begun, for there immediately arises the question of the relations of one term to the others. There have been few attempts at constructing a coherent system; and those that are coherent are not comprehended. In view of this Euroclydon of misunderstanding it is clearly necessary to establish a fundamental language. I saw this fact in my twenties. My extended travels throughout the world had brought me into contact with religious and philosophical thinkers of every shade of opinion: and the more I knew the greater became the confusion. I understood, with bitter approval, the outburst of the aged Fichte: "If I had my life to live again, the first thing I would do would be to invent an entirely new syatem of symbols whereby to convey my ideas." As a matter of fact, certain people, notably Raymond Lully, have attempted this great work.

I discussed this question with Bhikkhu Ananda Metteya (Allan Bennett) in 1904. He professed himself completely satisfied with the Buddhist terminology. I could not concur with his opinion. Firstly, the actual words are barbarously long, impossibly so for the average European. Secondly, an understanding of the system demands complete acquiescence in the Buddhist doctrines. Thirdly, the meaning of the terms is not, as my venerable colleague maintained, as clear and comprehensive as could be wished. There is much pedantry, much confusion, and much disputed matter. Fourthly, the terminology is exclusively psychological. It takes no account of extra-Buddhistic ideas; and it bears little relation to the general order of the universe. It might be supplemented by Hindu terminology. But to do that would immediately introduce elements of controversy. We should at once be lost in endless discussions as to whether Nibbana was Nirvana or not: and so on for ever.

The system of the Qabalah is superficially open to the last objection. But its real basis is perfectly sound. We can easily discard the dogmatic interpretation of the Rabbins. We can refer everything in the Universe to the system of pure number whose symbols will be intelligible to all rational minds in an indentical sense. An the relations between these symbols are fixed by nature. There is no particular point—for most ordinary purposes—of discussing whether 49 is or is not the square of 7.

Such was the nature of the considerations that led me to adopt the Tree of Life as the basis of the magical alphabet. The 10 numbers and the 22 letters of the Hebrew alphabet, with their traditional and rational correspondences (taking into consideration their numerical and geometrical interrelations) afford us a coherent systematic groundwork sufficiently rigid for our foundation and sufficiently elastic for our superstructure.

But we must not suppose that we know anything of the Tree *a priori*. We must not work towards any other type of central Truth than the nature of these symbols in themselves. The object of our work must be, in fact, to discover the nature and powers of each symbol. We must clothe the mathematical nakedess of each prime idea in a many-coloured carment of correspondences with every department of thought.

Our first task is thus to consider what we are to mean by the word number. I have deal with this in my commentary to Verse 4, Chapter I, of *The Book of the Law* "Every number is infinite: there is no difference."*

The student should be very thoroughly into the question of transfinite number. Let him consult the *Introduction to Mathematical Philosophy* of the Hon. Bertrand Russell in a reverent but critical spirit. In particular, in the light of my note on number, the whole conception of Aleph Zero[†] should give him a fairly clear idea of the essential paradoxes of the magical interpretation of the idea of number, and especially of the equation $0 = 2$ which I have devised to explain the universe, and to harmonise the antinomies which it presents us at every turn.

Our present state of understanding is far from perfect. It is evidently impossible to obtain a clear notion of each of the primes if only because their number is Aleph Zero.

---

* This commentary is including in the present volume, see "What is a 'Number' or 'Symbol'?" *infra*.

† [More usually written *aleph-null* or $\aleph_0$; the reference is to the infinite set of cardinal numbers. — T.S.]

The numbers 0 to 10, as forming the basis of the decimal system, may be considered as a microcosm of Aleph Zero. For they are endless, 10 representing the return to Unity by the reintroduction of Zero to continue the series in a manner progressively complex, each term representing not only itself in its relation with its neighbours, but the combination of two or more numbers of the first decad. That is, until we reach numbers whose factors are all (except unity) greater than 10; as $143 = (11 \times 13)$. But this necessity to consider such numbers as altogether beyond the first decad is only apparent; each prime being itself an elaboration in some sense or other of one or more of the original 0 to 10 series.* This at least may be regarded as conventionally true for immediate purposes of study. A number such as $3299 \times 3307 \times 3319$ may be regarded as a distant and not very important group of fixed stars. (Thus 13 is a "middle modulus" and 111 the "great modulus" of Unity. That is, the multiples of 13 and 111 explain the coefficients of their scales in terms of a more specialised idea of Unity. *E.g.* $26 = 2 \times 13$ represents the Dyad in a more specially connotated sense than 2 does; 888 describes the function of 8 in terms of the full meaning of 111, which is itself an elaborate account of the nature of Unity, including— for instance—the dogmatic mystery of the equation $3 = 1$.)

By repercussion, again, each larger correlative of any number of 0 to 10 expresses an extended idea of that number which must immediately be included in the fundamental conception thereof. For instance, having discovered that 120 can be divided by 5, we must henceforth think of 5 as the root of those ideas which we find in 120, as well as using our previous ideas of 5 as the key to our investigation of 120.

On the surface, it would appear that this mode of working could only lead to baffling contradictions and inextricable confusion; but to the mind naturally lucid and well trained to discrimination this misfortune does not occur. On the contrary, practice (which makes perfect) enables one to grasp intelligently and class coherently a far vaster congeries of facts than could possibly be assimilated by the most laborious feats of memorizing. Herbert Spencer has well explained the

* For the meaning of the primes from 11 to 97 see page 132.

psychology of apprehension. The excellence of any mind, considered merely as a storehouse of information, may be gauged by its faculty of re-presenting any required facts to itself by systematic classification into groups and sub-groups.

This present attempt at a magical alphabet is, in fact, a projection, both intensive and extensive, of this system to infinity. On the one hand, all possible ideas, are referred by progressive integrations to the pure numbers o to 10, and thence to 2, 1, and o. On the other, the connotations of o, 1, and 2 are extended, by progressive definitions, to include every conceivable idea on the plane of the Universe.

We are now in a position to consider the practical application of these ideas. As regards the numbers o to 10 of the Key-Scale, each one is a fundamental idea of a positive entity. Its nature is defined by the correspondences assigned to it in the various columns. Thus we may say that the God Hanuman, the Jackal, the Opal, Storax, Truthfulness and so on are all qualities inherent in the idea of 8.

With regard to the numbers 11 to 32 of the Key-Scale, they are not numbers at all in our sense of the word.* They have been arbitrarily assigned to the 22 paths by the compiler of the Sepher Yetzirah.†

There is not even any kind of harmony: nothing could be further

---

* [Except in column XLVIII, "Figures related to Pure Number" which refers the Swastika to line 17 (17 squares), the solid Greek Cross of 5 cubes to 22 (surface of 22 squares), *etc.* — T.S.]

† [The first paragraph of the *Sepher Yetzirah* declares (Westcott trans.): "In two and thirty most occult and wonderful paths of wisdom did JAH the Lord of Hosts engrave his name: God of the armies of Israel, ever-living God, merciful and gracious, sublime, dwelling on high, who inhabiteth eternity. He created this universe by the three Sepharim, Number, Writing, and Speech." The second paragraph begins "Ten are the numbers, as are the Sephiroth, and twenty-two the letters, these are the Foundation of all things." from which it is usually inferred that the 32 Paths are the ten numbers and 22 letters. The text "The Thirty-Two Paths of Wisdom" which gives a title and symbolic description of each 'Path' ("The First Path is called the Admirable or the Concealed Intelligence &c.") is a later appendix. Further, the arrangement of the Tree of Life with the 22 letters as 'paths' connecting the 10 numbers is itself *much* later than the *Seph. Yetz.*; the form used by Crowley, the Golden Dawn and most other Western occultists is believed to be a slight modification (with regard to proportion) of a design due to Athanasius Kircher, a 17th century Christian Cabalist. — T.S.]

from the idea of 29 than the sign of Pisces. The basic idea had better be considered the letter of the Hebrew Alphabet; and the correspondence of each with fairly comprehensive definitions such as the Tarot Trumps is very close and necessary. (It will be noticed that certain Alphabets, espcially the Coptic, have more than 22 letters. These additional symbols fill up the Tree of Life when attributed to the Sephiroth.*) The numerical value of the letters does however represent a real and important relation. But these numbers are not quite the same as the original sephirotic numbers. For instance, althought Beth = 2, = Mercury, and Mercury is part of the the idea of Chokmah = 2, the one 2 is not identical with the other. For Mercury, in itself, is not a Sephira. It is not a positive emanation in the necessary sequence in the scale 0 to 10. For Beth is the Path which joins Kether and Binah, 1 and 3. Zayin = 7 is the path joining Binah, 3, and Tiphareth, 6. That is, they are not numbers in themselves, but expressions of relations between numbers according to a predetermined geometrical pattern.

Another class of number is of immense importance. It is the series usually expressed in Roman numbers which is printed on the Tarot Trumps. Here, with two exceptions, the number is invariable one less than that of the letters of the alphabet, when they are numbered according to their natural order from 1 to 22.† These numbers are very nearly of the same order of idea as those of the numerical value of the letters; but they represent rather the active magical energy of the number than its essential being.

To return to the pure Sephiroth, the numbers 0, 1, 2, 3, 5 and 7 are primes, the others combinations of these primes. Here we have already the principle of equilibrium between the simple and the complex. At the same time there is an inherent virtue in the compound numbers as

---

* [Notice Aleister does not attempt to fit Devanagari, which has still more distinct letters than Coptic, into the scheme. — T.S.]

† [This statement does not take into account the Hé-Tzaddi reversal, since in the 777 scheme Crowley gave Strength, referred to Teth, the ninth letter, the number XI, and Justice, referred to the twelfth letter, Lamed, the number VIII. This agrees with the traditional numbering of the Trumps but throws the attribution to the Hebrew alphabet out of order. — T.S.]

such which makes it improper to think of them as merely combinations from their mathematical elements. Six is an idea in itself, a "Ding an sich."* The fact that $6 = 2 \times 3$ is only one of its properties. Similar remarks apply to the numbers about 10, but here the importance of the primes as compared to that of the compound numbers is much greater. Few compound numbers appear in the present state of our knowledge in themselves as distinguished from the value of their mathematical elements. We may however instance 93, 111, 120, 210, 418, 666. But every prime is the expression of a quite definite idea. For instance 19 is the general feminine glyph, 31 the highest feminine trinity, a "great modulus" of Zero. 41 is the aspect of the feminine as a vampire force. 47 as dynamic and spasmodic, 53 as hedonogenous, 59 as claiming its complement, and so on.

Each prime number retains its peculiar significance in its multiples. Thus the number 23, a glyph of life, exhibits the lift of the Dyad in 46, etc. The significance of the primes has been carefully worked out, with fair accuracy in each case, up to 97. Above 100 only a few primes have been thoroughly investigated. This is because, by our present methods, such numbers can only be studied through their multiples. That is to say, if we wish to determine the nature of the number 17 we shall examine the series 34, 51, 68, etc., to see what words and ideas correspond to them. We shall establish a ratio $51:34 = 3:2$. From our knowledge of 3 and 2 we can compare the effect produced on them by the modulus 17. For instance, 82 is the number of the Angel of Venus and means a thing beloved; 123 means war, a plague, pleasure, violation; and 164 has the idea of cleaving, also of profane as opposed to sacred. The common element in these ideas is a danagerous fascination; whence we say that 41, the highest common factor, is the Vampire.†

But the above considerations, which would extend the letters of the magical alphabet to an infinity of symbols, are not properly pertinent to

---

* [German, "Thing in itself."]

† A dictionary giving the meanings by traditional Qabalah of the numbers from 1 to 1,000 with a few higher numbers is published in *The Equinox* I (8) under the title "Sepher Sephiroth sub figura D."

this essay. Our main object is convenience in communicating ideas. And this would be violated if we aimed too high. We can attain all our objectives for practical purposes by confining ourselves to the traditionally accepted scale of 32 paths, of 10 numbers and 22 letters. The only extension necessary is the inclusion of the Veils of the Negative, a matter of fundamental importance in the apodeictic structure of the Tree given in the structural diagram.* These Veils are useful in only a very few positive lists.

The numbers 31 and 32 must be duplicated because the letter Shin possesses two very distinct branches of idea, one connected with the element of Fire, and the other with that of Spirit. Also the letter Tau is referred both to the planet Saturn and the element Earth. This is a great defect in the system, theoretically. But the traditional attributions are so numerous and well defined that no remedy seems feasible. (In practice no serious trouble of any kind is caused by the theoretical confusion.)

One further difficulty has arisen owing to the discovery of the planets Neptune and Uranus. We have however tried to turn this into an advantage by including them with Primum Mobile in a Sephirotic arrangement of the planets. And the device has justified itself by enabling us to construct a perfectly symmetrical attribution for the rulings and exaltations of the Signs of the Zodiac.†

For the rest it need only be said, that, as in the case of most lines of study, the key to success is the familiarity conferred by daily practice.

---

* [The Tree of Life diagram originally published in *777*, in common with that in the present edition, did not in fact show the Veils. See rather the diagrams from *The Book of Thoth* (reproduced in chapter 65 of *Magick Without Tears*). — T.S.]

† [This was written prior to the discovery of Pluto. Crowley's intermediate arrangement of the Planets to the Sephirothic scheme referred Neptune to Kether and Uranus to Chokmah; in addition an arrangement of "Superior Planetary Governers" set Uranus over the Kerubic signs, Neptune over the Mutables and the Primum Mobile over the Cardinals. In *The Book of Thoth*, post the discovery of Pluto, the final attributions of the Planets to Sephiroth was buried away in the description of ATU XXI: it referred Pluto to Kether, Neptune to Chokmah and Uranus to Daath. Pluto was now the 'Superior Planetary Governer' of the Kerubic signs, and the scheme of 'planets exalted in signs' had been filled out with the outer planets and Caput and Cauda Draconis. See "Various Arrangements," *supra*, and col. CXXXIX. — T.S.]

THE MEANING OF THE PRIMES
FROM 11 TO 97

11. The general number of magick, or energy tending to change.
13. The scale of the highest feminine unity; easily transformed to secondary masculine ideas by any male component; or, the unity resulting from love.
17. The masculine unity. (Trinity of Aleph, Vau, Yod.)
19. The feminine glyph.
23. The glyph of life—of nascent life.
29. The magick force itself, the masculine current.
31. The highest feminine trinity—zero through the glyph of the circle.
37. The unity itself in its balance trinitarian manifestation.
41. The yoni as a vampire force, sterile.
43. A number of orgasm—especially the male.
47. The yoni as dynamic, prehensile, spasmodic, etc. Esprit de travail.
53. The yoni as an instrument of pleasure.
59. The yoni calling for the lingam as ovum, menstruum, or alkili.
61. The negative conceiving of itself as positive.
67. The womb of the mother containg the twins.
71. A number of Binah. The image of nothingness and silence which is a fulfilment of the aspiration.
73. The feminine aspect of Chokmah in his phallic function.
79. [omitted]
83. Consecration: love in its highest form: energy, freedom, amrita, aspiration. The root of the idea of romance plus religion.
89. A number of sin—restriction. The wrong kind of silence, that of the Black Brothers.
97. A number of Chesed as water and as father.

WHAT IS QABALAH?

Qabalah is:—

a. A language fitted to describe certain classes of phenomena, and to express certain classes of ideas which escape regular phraseology. You might as well object to the technical terminology of chemistry.

b. An unsectarian and elastic terminology by means of which it is possible to equate the mental processes of people apparently diverse owing to the constraint imposed upon them by the peculiarities of their literary expression. You might as well object to a lexicon, or a treatise on comparative religion.

c. A system of symbolism which enables thinkers to formulate their ideas with complete precision, and to find simple expression for complex thoughts, especially such as include previously disconnected orders of conception. You might as well object to algebraic symbols.

d. An instrument for interpreting symbols whose meaning has become obscure, forgotten or misunderstood by establishing a necessary connection between the essence of forms, sounds, simple ideas (such as number) and their spiritual, moral, or intellectual equivalents. You might as well object to interpreting ancient art by consideration of beauty as determined by physiological facts.

e. A system of classification of uniform ideas so as to enable the mind to increase its vocabulary of thoughts and facts through organizing and correlating them. You mights as well object to the mnemonic value of Arabic modifcations of roots.

f. An instrument for proceding from the known to the unknown on similar principles to those of mathematics. You might as well object to the use of $\sqrt{-1}$, x^4, etc.

g. A system of criteria by which the truth of correspondences may be tests with a view to criticizing new discoveries in the light of their coherence with the whole body of truth. You might as well object to judging character and status by education and social convention.

WHAT IS A "NUMBER" OR "SYMBOL"?*

The Book of the Law I, 4, defines the word "number." It may clarify the subject if we venture to paraphrase the text. The first statement "Every number is infinite" is, on the face of it, a contradiction in terms. But that is only because of the accepted idea of a number as not being a thing in itself but merely a term in series homogeneous in character. All orthodox mathematical argument is based on definitions involving this conception. For example, it is fundamental to admit the identity of 2 plus 1 with 1 plus 2. *The Book of the Law* presents an altogether different conception of the nature of number.

Mathematical ideas involve what is called a continuum, which is, superficially at least, of a different character to the physical continuum. For instance, in the physical continuum, the eye can distinguish between the lengths of one-inch stick and a two-inch stick, but not between these which measure respectively one thousand miles and one thousand miles and on inch, though the difference in each case is equally an inch. The inch difference is either perceptible or not perceptible, according to the conditions. Similarly, the eye can distinguish either the one-inch or the two-inch stick from one of an inch and a half. But we cannot continue this process indefinitely—we can always reach a point where the extremes are distinguishable from each other but their mean from neither of the extremes. Thus, in the physical continuum, if we have three terms, A, B, and C, A appears equal to B, and B to C, yet C appears greater than A. Our reason tells us that this conclusion is an absurdity, that we have been deceived by the grossness of our perceptions. It is useless for us to invent instruments which

* [This essay formed the bulk of the New Comment on *AL* I. 4. It was omitted by Israel Regardie in the edition of the Commentaries he published as *The Law is for All*. The present e-text was originally key-entered by W.E. Heidrick for o.t.o. — T.S.]

increase the accuracy of our observations, for though they enable us to distinguish between the three terms of our series, and to restore the theoretical Hierarchy, we can always continue the process of division until we arrive at another series: A', B', C', where A' and C' are distinguishable from each other, but where neither is distinguishable from B'.

On the above grounds, modern thinkers have endeavoured to create a distinction between the mathematical and the physical continuum, yet it should surely be obvious that the defect in our organs of sense, which is responsible for the difficulty, shows that our method of observation debars us from appreciating the true nature of things by this method of observation.

However, in the case of the mathematical continuum, its character is such that we can continue indefinitely the process of division between any two mathematical expressions so-ever, without interfering in any way with the regularity of the process, or creating a condition in which two terms become indistinguishable from each other. The mathematical continuum, moreover, is not merely a question of series of integral numbers, but of other types of numbers, which, like integers, express relations between existing ideas, yet are not measurable in terms of that series. Such numbers are themselves parts of a continuum of their own, which interpenetrates the series of integers without touching it, at least necessarily.

For example: the tangents of angles made by the separation of two lines from coincidence to perpendicularity, increases constantly from zero to infinity. But almost the only integral value is found at the angle of 45 degrees where it is unity.

It may be said that there is an infinite number of such series, each possessing the same property of infinite divisibility. The ninety tangents of angles differing by one degree between zero and ninety may be multiplied sixty fold by taking the minute instead of the degree as the co-efficient of the progression, and these again sixty fold by introducing the second to divide the minute. So on ad infinitum.

All these considerations depend upon the assumption that every number is no more than a statement of relation. The new conception, indicated by the *Book of the Law*, is of course in no way contradictory of the orthodox view; but it adds to it in the most practically important manner. A statistician computing the birth-rate of the eighteenth century makes no special mention of the birth of Napoleon. This does not invalidate his results; but it demonstrates how exceedingly limited is their scope even with regard to their own object, for the birth of Napoleon had more influence on the death-rate than another other phenomenon included in his calculations.

A short digression is necessary. There may be some who are still unaware of the fact, but the mathematical and physical sciences are in no sense concerned with absolute truth, but only with the relations between observed phenomena and the observer. The statement that the acceleration of falling bodies is thirty-two feet per second, is only the roughest of approximation at the best. In the first place, it applies to earth. As most people know, in the Moon the rate is only one-sixth as great. But, even on earth, it differs in a marked manner between the poles and the equator, and not only so, but it is affected by so small a matter as the neighborhood of a mountain.

It is similarly inaccurate to speak of "repeating" an experiment. The exact conditions never recur. One cannot boil water twice over. The water is not the same, and the observer is not the same. When a man says that he is sitting still, he forgets that he is whirling through space with vertiginous rapidity.

It is possibly such considerations that led earlier thinkers to admit that there was no expectation of finding truth in anything but mathematics, and they rashly supposed that the apparent ineluctability of her laws constitutes a guarantee of their coherence with truth. But mathematics is entirely a matter of convention, no less so than the rules of Chess or Baccarat. When we say that "two straight lines cannot enclose a space," we mean no more than we are unable to think of them as doing so. The truth of the statement depends, consequently, on that of the hypothesis that our minds bear witness to truth. Yet the insane man may be unable to think that he is not the victim of mysterious persecution. We find that no reason for believing him. It is useless to reply that mathematical truths receive universal consent, because they do not. It is a matter of elaborate and tedious training to persuade even the few people whom we teach of the truth of the simplest theorems in Geometry. There are very few people living who are convinced—or even aware—of the more recondite results of analysis. It is no reply to this criticism to say that all men can be convinced if they are sufficiently trained, for who is to guarantee that such training does not warp the mind?

But when we have brushed away these preliminary objections, we find that the nature of the statement itself is not, and cannot be, more than a statement of correspondences between our ideas. In the example chosen, we have five ideas; those of duality, of straightness, of a line, of enclosing, and of space. None of these are more than ideas. Each one is meaningless until it is defined as corresponding in a certain manner to certain other ideas. We cannot define any word soever, except by identifying it with two or more equally undefined words. To define it by a single word would evidently constitute a tautology.

We are thus forced to the conclusion that all investigation may be stigmatized as *obscurum per obscurium*. Logically, our position is even worse. We define A as BC, where B is DE, and C is FG. Not only does the process increase the number of our unknown quantities in Geometrical progression at every step, but we must ultimately arrive at a point where the definition of Z involves the term A. Not only is all argument confined within a vicious circle, but so is the definition of the terms on which any argument must be based.

It might be supposed that the above chain of reasoning made all conclusions impossible. But this is only true when we investigate the ultimate validity of our propositions. We can rely on water boiling at 100 degrees Centigrade,* although, for mathematical accuracy, water never boils twice running at precisely the same temperature, and although, logically, the term water is an incomprehensible mystery.

* In revising this comment, I note with amusement that it had escaped me that 100° C. is by definition the temperature at which water boils! I have seen it boil at about 84° C. on the Baltoro Glacier, and determined my height above sea-level by observing the boiling point so often that I had quite forgotten the original conditions of Celsius.

To return to our so-called axiom; Two straight lines cannot enclose a space. It has been one of the most important discoveries of modern mathematics, that this statement, even if we assume the definition of the various terms employed, is strictly relative, not absolute; and that common sense is impotent to confirm it as in the case of the boiling water. For Bolyai, Lobatschewsky, and Riemann have shown conclusively that a consistent system of geometry can be erected on any arbitrary axiom soever. If one chooses to assume that the sum of the interior angles of a triangle is either greater than or less than two right angles, instead of equal to them, we can construct two new systems of Geometry, each perfectly consistent with itself, and we possess no means soever of deciding which of the three represents truth.

I may illustrate this point by a simple analogy. We are accustomed to assert that we go from France to China, a form of expression which assumes that those countries are stationary, while we are mobile. But the fact might be equally well expressed by saying that France left us and China came to us. In either case there is no implication of absolute motion, for the course of the earth through space is not taken into account. We implicitly refer to a standard of repose which, in point of fact, we know not to exist. When I say that the chair in which I am sitting has remained stationary for the last hour, I mean only "stationary in respect to myself and my house." In reality, the earth's rotation has carried it over one thousand miles, and the earth's course some seventy thousand miles, from its previous position. All that we can expect of any statement is that it should be coherent with regard to a series of assumption which we know perfectly well to be false and arbitrary.

It is commonly imagined, by those who have not examined the nature of the evidence, that our experience furnishes a criterion by which we may determine which of the possible symbolic representations of Nature is the true one. They suppose that Euclidian Geometry is in conformity with Nature because the actual measurements of the interior angles of a triangle tell us that their sum is in fact equal to two right angles, just as Euclid tells us that theoretical considerations declare to be the case. They forget that the instruments which we use for our measurements are themselves conceived of as in conformity with the principles of Euclidian Geometry. In other words, them measure ten yards with a piece of wood about which they really known nothing but that its length is one-tenth of the ten yards in question.

The fallacy should be obvious. The most ordinary reflection should make it clear that our results depend upon all sorts of condition. If we inquire, "What is the length of the thread of quicksilver in a thermometer?", we can only reply that it depends on the temperature of the instrument. In fact, we judge temperature by the difference of the coefficients of expansion due to heat of the two substances, glass and mercury.

Again, the divisions of the scale of the thermometer depend upon the temperature of boiling water, which is not a fixed thing. It depends on the pressure of the earth's atmosphere, which varies (according to time and place) to the extent of over twenty per cent. Most people who talk of "scientific accuracy" are quite ignorant of elementary facts of this kind.

It will be said, however, that having defined a yard as the length of a certain bar deposited in the Mint in London, under given conditions of temperature and pressure, we are at least in a position to measure the length of other objects by comparison, directly or indirectly, with that standard. In a rough and ready way, that is more or less the case. But if it should occur that the length of things in general were halved or doubled, we could not possibly be aware of the other so-called laws of Nature. We have no means so-ever of determining even so simple a matter as to whether one of two events happens before or after the other.

Let us take an instance. It is well known that the light of the sun requires some eight minutes to reach the earth. Simultaneous* phenomena in the two bodies would therefore appear to be separated in time to that extent; and, from a mathematical standpoint, the same discrepancy theoretically exists, even if we suppose the two bodies in

* Simultaneity, closely considered, possesses no meaning soever. See A.S. Eddington, *Space, Time and Gravitation*, 51.

question to be only a few yards one more remote than the other. Recent consideration of these facts has show the impossibility of determining the fact of priority, so that it may be just as reasonable to assert that a dagger-thrust is caused by a wound as vice versa. Lewis Carroll has an amusing parable to this effect in *Through the Looking-Glass*, which work, by the way, with its predecessor, is packed with examples of philosophical paradox.*

We may now return to our text "Every number is infinite." The fact that every number is a term in a mathematical continuum is no more an adequate definition than if we were to describe a picture as Number So-and-So in the catalogue. Every number is a thing in itself,† possessing an infinite number of properties peculiar to itself.

Let us consider, for a moment, the numbers 8 and 9. 8 is the number of cubes measuring one inch each way in a cube which measures two inches each way; while 9 is the number of squares measuring one inch each way in a square measuring three inches each way. There is a sort of reciprocal correspondence between them in this respect.

By adding one to eight, we obtain nine, so that we might define unity as that which has the property of transforming a three-dimensional expansion of two into a two-dimensional expansion of three. But if we add unity to nine, unity appears as that which has the power of trans-forming the two-dimensional expansion of three aforesaid into a mere

---

* If I strike a billiard ball, and it moves, both my will and its motion have causes long antecedent to the act. I may consider both my Work and its reaction as twin effects of the eternal Universe. The moved arm and ball are part of a state of the Cosmos which resulted necessarily from its momentarily previous state, and so, back for ever. Thus, my Magical Work is only on of the cause-effects necessarily concomitant with the cause-effects which set the ball in motion. I may therefore regard the act of striking as a cause-effect of my original Will to move the ball, though necessarily previous to its motion. But the case of Magical work is not quite analogous. For I am such that I am compelled to perform Magick in order to make my Will to prevail; so that the cause of my doing the Work is also he cause of the ball's motion, and there is no reason why one should precede the other, See *Book 4*, Part III, for a full discussion. (Since writing the above, I have been introduced to *Space, Time and Gravitation*, where similar arguments are adduced.)

† I regret to find myself in disagreement with the Hon. Bertrand Russell with regard to the conception of the nature of Number.

oblong measuring 5 by 2. Unity thus appears as in possession of two totally different properties. Are we then to conclude that it is not the same unity? How are we to describe unity, how know it? Only by experiment can we discover the nature of its action on any given number. In certain minor respects, this action exhibits regularity. We know, for example, that it uniformly transforms an odd number into an even one, and vice versa, but that is practically the limit of what we can predict as to its action.

We can go further, and state that any number soever possesses this infinite variety of powers to transform any other number, even by the primitive process of addition. We observe also how the manipulation of any two numbers can be arranged so that the result is incommensurable with either, or even so that ideas are created of a character totally incompatible with our original conception of numbers as a series of positive integers. We obtain unreal and irrational expressions, ideas of a wholly different order, by a very simple juxtaposition of such apparently comprehensible and commonplace entities as integers.

There is only one conclusion to be drawn from these various considerations. It is that the nature of every number is a thing peculiar to itself, a thing inscrutable and infinite, a thing inexpressible, even if we could understand it.

In other words, a number is a soul, in the proper sense of the term, an unique and necessary element in the totality of existence.

We may now turn to the second phrase of the text: "there is no difference." It must strike the student immediately that this is, on the face of it, a point blank contradiction of all that has been said above. What have we done but insist upon the essential difference between any two numbers, and show that even their sequential relation is little more than arbitrary, being indeed rather a convenient way of regarding them for the purpose of coordinating them with out understanding than anything else? On a similar principle, we number public vehicles or telephones without implication even of necessary sequence. The appellation denotes nothing beyond membership of a certain class of objects, and is indeed expressly chosen to avoid being entangled in considerations of any characteristics of the individual so designated except that cursory designation.

When it is said that there is no difference between numbers (for in this sense I think we must understand the phrase), we must examine the meaning of the word 'difference.' Difference is the denial of identity in the first place, but the word is not properly applied to discriminate between objects which have no similarity. One does not ask, "What is the difference between a yard and a minute?" in practical life. We do ask the difference between two things of the same kind. The *Book of the Law* is trying to emphasize the doctrine that each number is unique and absolute. Its relations with other numbers are therefore in the nature of illusion. They are the forms of presentation under which we perceive their semblances; and it is to the last degree important to realize that these semblances only indicate the nature of the realities behind them in the same way in which the degrees on a thermometric scale indicate heat. It is quite unphilosophical to say that 50 degrees Centigrade is hotter than 40 degrees. Degrees of temperature are simply conventions invented by ourselves to describe physical states of a totally different order; and, while the heat of a body may be regarded as an inherent property of its own, our measure of that heat in no way concerns it.

We use instruments of science to inform us of the nature of the various objects which we wish to study; but our observations never reveal the thing as it is in itself. They only enable us to compare unfamiliar with familiar experiences. The use of an instrument necessarily implies the imposition of alien conventions. To take the simplest example: when we say that we see a thing, we only mean that our consciousness is modified by its existence according to a particular arrangement of lenses and other optical instruments, which exist in our eyes and not in the object perceived. So also, the fact that the sum of 2 and 1 is three, affords us but a single statement of relations symptomatic of the presentation to us of those numbers.

We have, therefore, no means soever of determining the difference between any two numbers, except in respect of a particular and very limited relation. Furthermore, in view of the infinity of every number, it seems not unlikely that the apparent differences observed by us would tend to disappear with the disappearance of the arbitrary conditions which we attach to them to facilitate, as we think, our examination. We may also observe that each number, being absolute, is the centre of its universe, so that all other numbers, so far as they are related to it, are its appanages. Each number is, therefore, the totality of the universe, and there cannot be any difference between one infinite universe and another. The triangle ABC may look very different from the standpoints of A, B, and C respectively; each view is true, absolutely; yet it is the same triangle.

The above interpretation of the text is of a revolutionary character, from the point of view of science and mathematics. Investigation of the lines here laid down will lead to the solution of these grave problems which have so long baffled the greatest minds of the world, on account of the initial error of attaching them on lines which involve self-contradiction. The attempt to discover the nature of things by a study of the relations between them is precisely parallel with the ambition to obtain a finite value of π. Nobody wishes to deny the practical value of the limited investigations which have so long preoccupied the human mind. But it is only quite recently that even the best thinkers have begun to recognize that their work was only significant within a certain order. It will soon be admitted on all hands that the study of the nature of things in themselves is a work for which the human reason is incompetent; for the nature of reason is such that it must always formulate itself in proportions which merely assert a positive or negative relation between a subject and a predicate. Men will thus be led to the development of a faculty, superior to reason, whose apprehension is independent of the hieroglyphic representations of which reason so vainly makes use.* This then will be the foundation of the true spiritual science which is the proper tendency of the evolution of man. This Science will clarify, without superseding, the old; but it will free men from the bondage of mind, little by little, just as the old science has freed them from the bondage of matter.

* See "Eleusis," A. Crowley, *Collected Works*, Vol. III, Epilogue

Transcriber's notes

[The work as presented here is currently incomplete: owing to my complete ignorance of Arabic, one column (the Princes of the Jinn) and some endnote material (the 99 names of God) in that language have not been key-entered. Further proof reading is probably required.]

THIS ELECTRONIC EDITION of *777 Revised* was prepared from the version printed in *777 and other Qabalistic Writings* (originally published as *The Qabalah of Aleister Crowley*). As far as I can tell this was a facsimile from the 1955 first edition of *777 Revised*; while Crowley's original Preface was re-set in the 1955 edition, the Tables of Correspondence, Crowley's notes thereon, and the appendix giving the trigrams and hexagrams of the *I Ching* were (with minor exceptions) in their turn straight facsimiles from the original 1909 edition of *777*.

The present edition includes all the material from *777 Revised* [with the exception of Arabic material as noted above.]

The 11 columns (CLXXXIV – CXCIV) added in *777 Revised* were originally appended at the end of Table VI. Six were explanatory of or supplementary to existing columns: (*e.g.* numerations of Greek and Arabic letters, transliterations or translations; the "magical formulæ" column was specifically referred to the column of magical weapons); these have been placed immediately after the appropriate column. The others have been appended to the end of the appropriate table. While they are hence "out of sequence" I feel this is unlikely to cause confusion as these additional columns are rarely if ever directly referenced by number in other works.

Very few of the columns in table IV had any attributions to line o. This line has thus been omitted to save space in most of the blocks of columns making up that table.

Additional correspondences as mentioned in Crowley's remarks on the various columns have been inserted into the appropriate columns in double square brackets [[like this]].

Also added are:
* Names and numeration of Coptic letters.
* Transliterations of most Hebrew names. The more obscure of these are taken from *Godwin's Cabalistic Encyclopedia* (3rd edition, Llewellyn, 1994), henceforth 'Godwin'.
* Translations of col. LXXVI and CXIX.
* Crowley's scheme of "Superior Planetary Governers" from *Magick in Theory and Practice*, which refers the outer planets to the Quaternions of the Signs.

The other additional materials from *777 Revised* have been included in what seemed to be appropriate places within this text. They are indicated by asterisks in the main Table of Contents. Most were key-entered by myself, the exception being "What is a 'Number'" which was extracted from an electronic text of the Commentaries on *Liber AL* found online, entered by Bill Heidrick and others.

I have made no attempt to preserve the original pagination. While Crowley occasionally referenced *777* by page number, such references are usually coupled with reference to the column. For ease of reading, columns are arranged from left to right across a single page. Obvious typos have been corrected; other questionable readings are noted below.

Footnotes in square brackets are by the present transcriber; others are either by Crowley or the original editors of *777 Revised*. Some lengthy notes to the original introduction, tables of correspondence and the notes on the tables from the first edition follow.

Endnotes

Notes to Crowley's Preface

[1] S.L. "MacGregor" Mathers.

[2] A crude early attempt to tabulate the data of Comparative Religion may be found in the table which forms appendix IV of *Rivers of Life* by J.G.R. Forlong (1883).

[3] The reference is probably to the *Heptameron seu elementa magica*, a 16th-century Grimoire of planetary magick (published with the *Fourth Book* of pseudo-Agrippa) deriving in part from the Solomonic cycle and in part from the *Liber Juratus* or *Sworn Book of Honorius*, a medieval work on magick (not to be confused with the early modern *Grimoire of Honorius* falsely attributed to the third Pope of that name). Its attribution to Pietro d'Abano (1253-1316) is generally recognised as spurious. The uncontested works of d'Abano do deal in part with astrological images and the medical / talismanic use of the same (*vide* Walker, *Spiritual and Demonic Magic* and Yates, *Giordano Bruno*), and he is occasionally cited as an authority by Renaissance writers such as Ficino and Agrippa; the material specifically attributed to d'Abano in *777* is from the *Heptameron*, although the images of the decans may be from his genuine works.

[4] A reference to the Golden Dawn. After swearing a long and tortuously phrased Oath of Secrecy, the Neophyte was issued a "Knowledge Lecture" which consisted of the names and symbols of the Elements, Planets and Signs along with the Hebrew Alphabet and the names of the Sephiroth in Hebrew.

[5] The *Lemegeton* is a 17th-century compilation, probably English, of magical texts attributed to Solomon. The first book, *Goetia*, describes 72 "Evil Spirits" and gives instructions for evoking them (it derives variously from the *Key of Solomon*, the *Heptameron*, the *Fourth Book* of pseudo-Agrippa and the *Pseudomonarchia Dæmonum* published by Wier). Crowley published an edition in 1904, from a text prepared by Mathers which had circulated in MS. in the Golden Dawn. In cols. CLV – CLXVI the spirits are referred to the Decans by day and night.

The second book, *Theurgia Goetia*, lists 31 principal spirits, with an astronomical number of subordinates of whom few are named; of the 31, 20 are referred to the points of the compass and the other 11 are said to wander and have no fixed place. They are said to be partly evil and party good, hence the apparently oxymoronic title. It is possible that the *Theurgia-Goetia* was based on the *Steganographia* of Trithemius by someone who did not realise that the latter was primarily a work of cryptography.

The third book, *Ars Paulina*, contains a catalogue of Angels for the 12 hours of the day and night, and for the 12 signs and 360 degrees of the Zodiac; they are also attributed to the seven classical Planets.

The fourth book, *Ars Almadel*, is probably of medieval origin: it divides up the powers it summons into four "Altitudes", seemingly referred to the cardinal points of the Zodiac.

The "fifth book of the Lemegeton", *Ars Nova*, is rather a kind of appendix which appears in one MS. where it occupies one and a half sides of a single folio leaf: it contains an extended prayer associated with the names on the circle and triangle of the *Goetia*, possibly intended to be spoken while drawing these, along with a short and garbled conjuration containing some highly corrupt Hebrew names, probably also connected with the *Goetia* as it mentions the brazen vessel; and finally, a lengthy curse targetted at anyone who steals the book.

The *Ars Nova* is sometimes confused with the *Ars Notoria* (Notary Art) attributed to Solomon, which latter rather appears to be a medieval magical derivative of classical art of memory, based around the contemplation of images or *notæ* while repeating prayers. The *Ars Notoria* was condemned by Aquinas (cited in Yates, *Art of Memory*) and various Renaissance writers such as Erasmus and Agrippa (in *De vanitate &c.*); Robert Turner produced an English translation which was made less than useful by the omission of the figures: this translation has been incorporated into some later MSS. and printed editions of the *Lemegeton*.

[6] In *The Book of the Sacred Magic of Abramelin the Mage* (lib. II cap. XIX) are tabulated the names of various Evil Spirits: chief among these are the "Four Princes and Superior Spirits", to wit Lucifer, Leviathan, Satan and Belial who may perhaps be referred to the Elements (I would suggest Fire, Water, Air, Earth respectively); immediately below these are eight "Sub-Princes", namely Oriens, Paimon, Ariton, Amaimon (*vide 777* col. LXVIII), Astarot, Magot, Asmodee and Beelzebud (*sic*); a total of 316 named spirits are listed below the eight Sub-Princes, some subject to one, some shared between two or more.

[7] The Book of the Concourse of the Forces is the title of a collection of Golden Dawn papers loosely based on the "Enochian" material which emerged from the ceremonial skrying of John Dee and Edward Kelly. Crowley later published a terse and incomplete abstract of this material as "A brief abstract of the symbolic representation of the Universe" in *Equinox* I (7-8). See also Regardie (ed.) *The Golden Dawn*, vol. IV.

[8] This would not be a view generally shared by most serious practitioners and students of Dee and Kelly's magick. Unless Crowley is talking about the G.D. version of "Enochian Magic" in which case he has a point.

Tree of Life diagram

4 Planes: the first consists solely of Kether; the second of Chokmah and Binah; the third of Chesed through to Yesod; the fourth of Malkuth only. These are identified by some with the Four Worlds. 3 Pillars / 7 Planes: see col. XII. 7 palaces: see col. LXXXVII et seq.

Notes to Tables of Correspondence

Table I (the whole scale)

Col. IV. The Arabic, as far as I can tell, means "He is God and there is no other God than he, هو being taken as equivalent to the Hebrew הוא.

Col. VIII. The numbers after the Qliphoth of the Sephiroth represent which of the seven "palaces" they are referred to: see the arrangements in Col. LXXXVIII et. seq. Transliterations are as given in Crowley's remarks on this column in *777 Revised*, although a few have been altered where

they are not consistent with the Hebrew spelling.

Col. XIV. These represent G.D. attributions, before Crowley changed the titles of a number of the Trumps in *The Book of Thoth* and exchanged the attributions of the Star and Emperor based on AL I.57.

Col. XIX. Transliterations of Egyptian names have been left as in the first edition. These differ from both modern transliterations and those employed by early 20th-century writers such as Budge.

Line 1: Asar is better known by the Hellenized form Osiris; Asar-un-Nefer ("Osiris the beautiful") was a epiphet or title of this god. Hadith in this line (also Hadit in line 0) is not a historical Egyptian deity but refers to the entity described in cap. II of *The Book of the Law*; the name is a garbled or corrupt form of Heru-Behutet (Horus of Behutet), a solar-martial form of Horus symbolized by the winged disk. Heru-Ra-Ha is not a historical Egyptian deity but is mentioned in cap. III of *The Book of the Law* and is said to combine Hoor-par-Kraat (Horus the Child) and Ra-Hoor-Khuit (Ra-Horus of the Two Horizons).

Line 6: "On" was not an Egyptian deity but a transliteration into Hebrew (אן or און) of the name of the Egyptian solar cult-centre called Heliopolis by the Greeks. The confusion arose through a misreading by Freemasons of Genesis XLI, 45 and 50 where Joseph married "Asenath daughter of Poti-phera priest of On." ON spelt עין as a formula is another matter entirely; see Col. CLXXXVII. Hrumachis is probably a variant spelling of Harmachis (Hor-Maku), said by Budge (*Gods of the Egyptians* vol. I p. 470) to be the Greek name for Heru-Khuti, Horus of the two horizons, who represented the sun from sunrise to sunset.

Line 13: Chomse also spelt Khons or Khensu. In one legend (cited by Budge, *op. cit.* I, 448) he is said to be the son of the cat goddess Bast who was also associated with the moon.

Lines 16, 32-bis: Ahapshi is the Apis Bull (GD Coptic spelling). Ameshet is Amset (or Mestha), one of the Children of Horus.

Line 17: The Rekti goddesses and Merti goddesses both appear to have been specific titles or epithets of Isis and Nephthys. See above for Heru-Ra-Ha.

Line 19: Pasht (according to Budge, *op. cit.* I, 517) is Pekh or Pekhit, a minor lioness goddess. Mau is onomatopœic Egyptian for 'cat' and appears to have been an epithet of Ra.

Line 22: Ma more usually spelt Maat or Ma'at.

Lines 23, 31: Auramoth and Thoum-aesh-neith were never Egyptian deities but were names constructed on Qabalistic principles by the Golden Dawn to refer to water and fire; similarly the name Tarpesheth (Tharpesht) is unknown prior to G.D. material, although she appears to be a hybrid of Bast and Sekhet. Hekar is possible Hequet or Hekt.

Line 24: Typhon was a Titan in Greek myth (son of Tartaros and Gaia), probably a personification of destructive forces of nature, who was identified with Set in late classical times. Add Selket, whose symbol was the scorpion. The attribution of Khephra is explained by Crowley's remarks on this line in the "Animals" column.

Line 25: Add Neith (Net) who is traditionally depicted with a bow and arrows.

Line 26: Khem is identified by Budge (*op. cit.*, I, 97) with the phallic god Min or Amsu, and was identified by the Greeks with Pan.

Line 28: Ahephi is Hāpi, one of the Children of Horus.

Line 29: Add Hequet (Hekt).

Line 31: Kabeshunt is probably Qebhsennuf, one of the Children of Horus.

Line 32: Mako (or Makou), son of Set, is a mythological crocodile; the name appears in the Harris Magic Papyrus (19th or 20th Dynasty), in the course of a charm against crocodiles addressed to Shu.

In the Golden Dawn Z1 paper the Children of Horus or Canopic Gods had 'invisible stations' in the corners of the Temple. The most immediate source for the elemental attributions, though, is

the Golden Dawn paper on "Enochian Chess" where the four pawns of each side are referred to these God-forms. It is not clear why Crowley omitted Tuamutef for Water (a G.D. Coptic form of this name is cited in connection with the "Eagle Kerub" in a ritual in *Equinox* I (3)).

In a myth recounted by Budge (*op. cit.* vol. I p. 158) these gods are said to have grasped the four pillars of heaven as sceptres: Amset the South, Hāpi the North, Tuamutef the East, and Qebhsennuf the West. They were also said to guard the Canopic Jars in which the internal organs of the deceased were preserved, and their G.D. attributions to the cross-quarters probably derive from a single find of an Egyptian tomb which had the four jars with the images of the gods disposed thus.

Col. XX.

Line 23: Possibly a G.D. Coptic spelling of Ashtoreth (Astarte, Asherah) who according to Budge (*op. cit.*) was worshipped in Egypt in the later dynastic period.

Line 25: A G.D. Coptic spelling of Aroueris.

Col. XXI. All this is derived from the famous speech in cap. 42 of the *Book of the Dead*. Some minor errors have been corrected. The Planets are referred to the face according to the attributions in Agrippa (tom. II cap. x); hence the duplication of left and right eye, ear and nostril.

Line 15: Budge has "hands."

Line 32 bis: *Alim Chayyim*, "the living Gods."

Col. XXIII. "Nothing and Neither P nor p'") and "Beaten and Scattered Corpse" each denote two different meditations.

Col. XXXIV.

Line 13: Add Selēnē who was a personification of the Moon as distinct from the goddesses with lunar aspects such as Artemis, Hekatē, etc. Similarly Helios was a personification of the Sun. See Betz (ed.) *The Greek Magical Papyri in Translation*.

Col. XXXV. Agrippa (*De occ. phil.* tom II cap xiv) in his "Orphic Scale of the Number Twelve" refers the twelve principle gods of Rome to the Zodiac:

♈ Pallas (Minerva)   ♎ Vulcan
♉ Venus   ♏ Mars
♊ Phoebus   ♐ Diana
♋ Mercury   ♑ Vesta
♌ Jupiter   ♒ Juno
♍ Ceres   ♓ Neptune.

Crowley omitted Jupiter and Phoebus from these for some reason.

Col. XXXVI. The Evangelists follow the traditional attribution to the Kerubim. Godwin gives the Apostles thus (he does not state his source):

♈ Matthias
♉ Thaddeus
♊ Simon
♋ John
♌ Peter
♍ Andew
♎ Bartholemew
♏ Phillip
♐ James son of Zebedee
♑ Thomas
♒ Matthew
♓ James son of Alpheus.

Stirling (*The Canon*, p. 102) gives a completely different arrangement.

Col. CLXXXVII. See *Magick in Theory and Practice* for a discussion of some of these formulæ. Another set of attributions of magical formulæ to the Tree of Life survives in one of Crowley's magical notebooks and may be studied in *Magick: Book 4 Parts I-IV* (editor's notes to Appendix V col. 34).

Line 0: LASTAL is not necessarily an error for LAShTAL (for which see *Liber V vel Reguli*) but may be a variant form, the ST representing the Coptic *sou*, identified with the Greek *stau* and attributed to Kether (see Col LI and *Magick*, loc. cit.). M . . . . M probably refers to MUAUM, said (in a letter from C.S. Jones to Frank Bennet) to be the Word of a Neophyte of A∴A∴, representing the whole course of the breath. Spelt מואים in Hebrew, it adds to 93 (it also contains a concealed *yod* in third place, not pronounced or counted in the numeration, which explains one of the dots in M . . . . M and the greenish-yellow coloured band in the glyph for the word in *Pyramidos*).

Lines 1-9: In *The Heart of the Master*, section *Aves* ('Birds'), nine magical formulæ are given as the voices of various symbolic birds, apparently referred to the Sephiroth 1-9, thus:
  1 (the Swan): AUMGN (one version has AUM)
  2 (the Phœnix): AL
  3 (the Raven): AMEN
  4 (the Eagle): SU
  5 (the Hawk): AGLA
  6 (the Pelican): IAO
  7 (the Dove): HRILIU
  8 (the Ibis): ABRAHADABRA
  9 (the Vulture): MU

Line 24: Possibly ON (*ayin nun*) could also be referred here.

Col. XLVI. Crowley's later attributions of the Taoist principles and the trigrams of the *I Ching* to the Sephiroth are given in *The Book of Thoth* (Appendix II, diagram 'The Chinese Cosmos') thus:
  0: Tao.
  1: Tao Teh.
  2: Yang.
  3: Yin.
  Daath: Khien.
  4: Tui.
  5: *Kăn*.
  6: Li.
  7: Kăn.
  8: Sun.
  9: Khân.
  10: Khwăn.

Col. XLVIII. Most of these refer to symbols appearing in Golden Dawn rituals.

Line 26: Possibly should read "Calvary Cross of 6, Solid" *i.e.* a cross composed of six cubes which will have a surface area of 26 squares.

Col L.

Line 31-bis: Add *Ire* (to Go). See *The Book of Thoth*, Appendix 2, diagram 8. Note S.V.A.T.I., *Sub Vmbra Alarum Tuarum Iehovah* (or Isis).

Col LI. This arrangement differs slightly from the G.D. attributions in Regardie (ed.), *Complete G.D.* (buried in the Ring and Disk paper), in that т and ө have been interchanged. In the printed edition of *777*, ℸ was given in line **1** as well as line **13**, and Ɛ in line **10** (**C** did not appear on the table). These have been corrected as compositor's errors; Ɛ has been placed in line **1** and **C** in line **10** in accordance with G.D. attributions. For each letter, 'upper case' and 'lower case' forms are shown; there is a certain amount of variation in the orthography of Coptic.

The three un-numbered columns are extracted in this instance from Appendix V to the 'Blue Brick' edition of *Magick*, in turn deriving from Crowley's magical notebooks. Numbers seem in most cases to be those of the equivalent Greek letter; the 'English equivalents' do not always represent the original phonetic value of the letters but rather refer to the transliterations employed in the Golden Dawn, where Coptic spellings of the names of various Egyptian Gods were constructed according to the Qabalistic attributions of the letters. The letter *sou* (Ɛ, ⲉ) did not historically have a phonetic value as such but was rather used to fill out the numbering scheme by standing for 6; whence it was identified with the obsolete Greek letter *stau* or *stigma* (ς) which was also used for number 6, and given the value 'st.'

Col LII. The letters are shown in their 'isolated' forms; since Arabic is written cursively, letter forms vary slightly depending on whether the letter appears on its own, or in the beginning, in the middle, or at the end of a word. The repetition of one letter in lines **9** and **10** appears to be deliberate.

Table II (the Elements)

Col. LXVI. The numerical value of each of these spellings gives the number in Col. LXV, which, rendered in Hebrew letters, gives the "secret name" in Col. LXIV.

Line **31**. Printed as יוד היה ויו היה, which adds to 82 rather than 72. The reading here is from Mathers' introduction to *Kaballah Unveiled*.

Col. LXXVI. The five *skandhas* are categories of mental phenomenon in Buddhist psychology. The translations are taken in this instance from the "Buddhist Dictionary" by Ven. Nyanatiloka, issued by the Buddhist Publication Society.

Table III (the Planets)

Col. LXXVIII.

Line **13**. Various spellings of this horrendous name have appeared in the literature, and as mentioned in Crowley's notes, this spelling can only be got to 3321 by counting the final ם as 700 rather than the more usual 600. Liber D had מלכא בתרשישים ועד ברוח שחרים, Malkah be-Tarshishim ve-A'ad be-Ruah Sheharim, which gives the required value without any fudging. The oldest known form (Agrippa, *op. cit.*, lib. II, cap. xxii) is עד ברוח שחקים מלכא בתרשיתים, Malkah be-Tarshithim A'ad be-Ruach Shechaqim.

Table IV (the Sephiroth)

Col. LXXXVIII. These originally given in Latin; I have translated them into English.

Col. XCII. The original had this in Latin; it was a slight garbling of the Vulgate of Isaiah VI, 2-3. I have translated it into English as it appeared.

Col. XCIV. Although headed "English of Palaces" this column was printed in Latin. The translations of the Seven Heavens are mostly from *Godwin's Cabalistic Encyclopedia*, s.v. "Heaven."

Col. CIII. This column originally printed in Latin (from *Kabbala Denudata*, tom. I, par. IV, fig xvi (P).).

Col. CVIII. For what it's worth (probably not much; see Crowley's note), here are transliterations of the Hebrew names in this column:

Line **2**. Samael ("poison of God" or "blind god"). סמאל = 131 = Παν.

Line **3**. Isheth Zanunim (Woman of Whoredom), said to be the wife of Samael. אשת זנונים = 864 = קרוש קדשים, Qadosh Qadshim, Holy of Holies. Doubtless there is an Arcanum concealed here, possibly along the lines of "you can prove anything with Gematria if you try hard enough."

Line **5**. Ashteroth. Historically a Middle Eastern goddess (Ishtar, Astarté, Asherah, *etc.*), denounced and maliciously mis-spelt by Old Testament writers and given an inexplicable sex change by medieval demonologists.

Line **6**. Chiva, the Beast; said to be the off-spring of Samael and Isheth Zanunim (see Mathers' introduction to *Kaballah Unveiled*, para 61). Only a hideous fudge (to wit (*a*) mis-spelling the name as אחיוה, (*b*) writing each letter out in full and (*c*) counting *hé* in full as הא rather than the more usual הה) can get this name to add to 666.

Line **7**. Asmodai. Appears in the apocryphal Book of Tobit. Sometimes also known by the Latinised form Asmodeus. The name is possibly a modification of Aeshma Deva, an evil spirit from Persian mythology.

Line **8**. Belial. Said to be the chief of the evil spirits in some late Jewish apocalyptic liter-ature (*e.g.* the Testament of the 12 Patriarchs), but in the Old Testament the name was a mere term of abuse meaning "masterless" or "worthless."

Line **9**. Lilith. She gets everywhere.

Line **10**. Naamah. The sister of Tubal-Cain (see Masonic symbolism); but in the *Zohar* she gets turned into another version of Lilith.

Col. CIX. Rather than use planetary symbols to distinguish the Kings and Dukes as in the printed edition, I have split this column. For Daath add King Bela son of Beor (בלע בן בעור) and Dukes Timnah (תמנע), Alvah (עלוה) and Jetheth (יתת).

Col. CX.

Line **1**. *Ruach Elohim Chayyim*, the Spirit of the Living Gods. The first edition of *777* had as a subtitle אחת רוח אלהים חיים, *Achath Ruach Elohim Chayyim* ("one [is] the Spirit of the Living Elohim"), a line from the *Sepher Yetzirah* which adds to *777*.

Cols. CXII – CXIII. These sets of attributions were extracted by the Golden Dawn from the first volume of *Kabbala Denudata*. The symbols in **7** and **8** apparently represent "hermaphroditic Brass."

Col. CXIV. The numbers are an addition; each password adds to the "mystic number" of the Sephirah corresponding. *Vide* Col. X.

Col. CXV. The entries in this column were originally given as initials only.

Col. CXIX. I have added translations, based on those in the "Buddhist Dictionary" (see note to col. LXXVI). In "Science and Buddhism," Crowley glosses Udha*kk*a as "Self-righteousness."

Col. CXXI. These are Golden Dawn titles. The A∴A∴ titles in the 1st order differ slightly; 0°=0° is Probationer, 1°=10° is Neophyte, 2°=9° Zelator and the "waiting" grade between Philosophus and Adeptus Minor is called Dominus Liminis.

Cols. CXXIX – CXXXII. These are the Angels of the Shem ha-Mephorash or 72-fold Divided Name of God, a full explanation of which would be beyond the scope of this footnote. See Godwin, *s.v.* "Shem ha-Mephorash." On each row, the name on the left rules the card in question by day, the one on the right by night.

Cols. CXXXIII – CXXXVI. Words in square brackets are the *Book of Thoth* keywords for these cards where these differ from the titles.

Table V (the Zodiac)

Col. CXXXIX. The outer planets – Uranus (♅), Nepture (♆) and Pluto (♇) and the Nodes of the Moon were not given in this table in *777*, but appeared in these positions in the table "The Essential Dignities of the Planets" in *The Book of Thoth* (reproduced in diagrammatic form in "Various Arrangements," p. 41).

Col. CXXXIXa. This data in this column appeared in Appendix V of *Magick*, with the title of col. CXXXIX erroneously placed at its head (*MTP* had "P.M." for *Primum Mobile* where this has Pluto, not then discovered). The scheme also appears in *The Book of Thoth*, appendix B.

Cols. CXLIX – CLI. Agrippa (tom. II cap. xxxvii) gives a somewhat different set of images for the decans, along with the significance of each. It is believed Agrippa derived from Latin translations of the *Picatrix*, a medieval Arabic work on magic. The images given here are close to those printed by Regardie in *Complete Golden Dawn*, and thus probably represent those circulating in the G.D. (possibly deriving from Petro d'Abano), though Regardie also gave the signification of each image (similar but not always identical to those in Agrippa).

Cols. CLV – CLXVI. I have added translit-erations of the names of the spirits and numbers according to the order in which they appear in the *Goetia*. Planetary symbols indicate the rank of the spirit and the material from which its seal is to be made (some spirits have two ranks), thus (the original text has the seals of Earls made in mixed copper and silver; Mathers suggests copper/silver or silver/mercury alloy for the Presidents):

Rank	Planet	Metal
Knight	Saturn	Lead
Prince	Jupiter	Tin
Earl	Mars	Iron
King	Sol	Gold
Duke	Venus	Copper
President	Mercury	Mercury (hmm...)
Marquis	Luna	Silver

In rendering the names of the demons into Hebrew, some suffixes like –ion, –ius, *etc.* have been dropped.

An alternative set of attributions and Hebrew spellings can be found in *The Sword and the Serpent* by Denning and Phillips, and *Godwin's Cabalistic Encyclopedia*.

Cols. CLXVII – CLXXI. A completely different set of names for the dekans and the gods referred to them may be found in Budge's *Gods of the Egyptians*, vol. ii pp 304-310. I am unaware of Crowley's source for these attributions: generally the names seem somewhat Hellenized.

Notes to Crowley's notes

[1] Because כח = *Koch*, Power, and כח is the "secret name" of Yetzirah (*vide* Col. LXIV).

[2] *i.e.*, the Hebrew word for "ten."

[3] The G.D. Qliphoth lecture (as published by Zalewski, etc.) has אבדרן, Abaddon; Crowley's reading matches that in *Kabbala Denudata* (tom. I par. IV fig. xvi (Y)); although this entity is there described as *innominatus*, 'nameless' or 'unnamed.'

[4] The print edition had כעמה; this has been assumed to be an error for Naamah or Nahemah (see also col. CVIII); the reading given follows Von Rosenroth (*loc. cit.*) which is the source for this as for so much else in *777*.

[5] "Rosicrucian Chess" is also known as "Enochian Chess" although its connection with Dee and Kelly's magick is tenuous at best; it is a four-handed game also used as a system of divination, loosely based on an ancient Indian game called Chaturanga, with pieces representing Egyptian Gods, played on an 8 by 8 board said to represent one of the four Watchtowers (with about half the squares omitted to get it the right size). For a more detailed account see Zalewski, *Enochian Chess of the Golden Dawn* (Llewellyn).

Rather than attempt to transliterate and then decipher the Coptic names given by Crowley (some of which I suspect are corrupt or misprinted) I will give the versions of these names as listed in Regardie (ed.), *Complete G.D.* (lib. X pp. 113-4). In many cases these are not reasonable transliterations of the names printed in *777*.

Fire:
Bishop: Toum.
Queen: Sati-Ashtoreth.
Knight: Ra.
Castle: Anouke (possibly Ankhet, a title of Isis)
King: Kneph (Khnemu).

Water:
Bishop: Hapimon (the Nile god)
Queen: Thouerist (Ta-urt the hippopotamus goddess)
Knight: Sebek
Castle: Shu
King: Osiris

Air:
Bishop: Shu
Queen: Knousou
Knight: Seb
Castle: Tharpesht (a G.D. amalgam of Bast and Sekhet)
King: Socharis (Seker; an early god who became identified with Ptah, and later with Osiris)

Earth:
Bishop: Aroueris
Queen: Isis
Knight: Hoori (Horus)
Castle: Nephthys
King: Aeshoori (*i.e.* Osiris again)

Pawns
Knight's pawn: Kabexnuv (Qebhsennuf)
Queen's Pawn: Tmoumathph (*sic*) (Tuamutef)
Bishop's Pawn: Ahepi (Hāpi)
Rook's Pawn: Ameshet (Mestha)

[6] I cannot identify the first three of these names. I believe the remaining four were intended to be G.D. Coptic spellings of Hapi (Ahephi), Tuamutef (Toumathph), Mestha (Ameshett) and Qebhsennuf (Kabexnuv), the Sons of Horus, and have corrected them accordingly.

[7] *De. occ. phil.* lib. I. cap xxiii. The following six chapters list various things said to be under the power of the other six classical planets. See also cap. xxii which gives general attributions for the planets and the theory behind all this, and cap. xxxii, "What things are under the Signs, the Fixed Stars, and their images."

[8] On typographic and chronological evidence this line was an addition in *777 Revised*.

[9] As noted above, this last is a fudge which was made necessary by someone miscopying the name of the Intelligence of the Intelligences of the Moon so it no longer added to 3321.

[10] The Golden Dawn lectures give a slightly different attribution of the fingers, based on the points of the Pentagram, thus: the thumb to Spirit, the index to Water, the medius to Fire, the third finger to Earth and the little finger to Air.

[11] In the Golden Dawn diagram (in turn derived from a figure in plate XVI in tom. i of von Rosenroth's *Kabbala Denudata*) from which Col. CVI. was derived, the seven Earths of Col. CIV. were also enclosed by the four seas. Godwin refers the Infernal Rivers to the Elements thus: Air, Cocytus; Water, Styx; Fire, Phlegethon; Earth, Acheron.

[12] "heled, concealed, and never revealed." See the Oath of an Entered Apprentice Freemason.

[13] The names appear in a supplement to the *Rituel de Haute Magie* as part of an "explanation" of the "Nuctemeron of Apollonius of Tyana." In cap. XVII of the *Rituel* Levi gives the names and characters of another 24 Zodiacal genii, two for each sign. The latter are here omitted.

[14] *i.e.*, the author of the *Heptameron* (see note to Preface on this point). But much of the following derives from the *Liber Juratus* in any case.

[15] I have reduced this into a single table to save space, representing each day and Angel with the corresponding planetary symbol.

[16] The names here have been conformed to the version of the *Heptameron* printed in the Lyons edition of Agrippa's *Opera*. Crowley, possibly because he was working from a corrupted copy, stated that none were given for Winter; although the names he gave for the Sun and Moon in Autumn were those referred to Winter by pseudo-Abano.

Appendix: the Yi King

Transliterations of Chinese names follow the system used by Legge in *Sacred Books of the East*, which is not in general current use. In particular, note that consonants have different phonetic values when italicised (*K* is "thin (tenuis) modified guttural consonant", *Kh* "aspirated thin modified guttural"). ă represents the 'neutral' vowel sound. Where Crowley has 'tz', Legge used a character something like a stylised 3; but as far as I can tell from the table of transliteration conventions, this is equivalent to the Hebrew **צ** (described helpfully as "Spiritus asperrimus 2" under dental consonants).

While this may be a little awkward and confusing, I would submit it is to be preferred to a transliteration scheme which manages to give the same transliteration for two different Chinese characters (*vide* the Wilhelm-Baynes *I Ching*, s.v. Hexagram 63).

The main traditional glosses to the trigrams are:

☰   Heaven, sky

☱   Water (marsh or lake)

☲   Fire, sun, lightning

☳   Thunder

☴   Wind and wood

☵   Water (rain, clouds, springs), moon

☶   Hill or mountain

☷   Earth

Additional traditional correspondences can be found in the "Eighth Wing" (Appendix V. in the Legge edition, "Shuo Kwa / Discussion of the Trigrams" in Part II of the Wilhelm-Baynes edition).

*** ***** ***